The Decision-Maker's Guide to Equity Compensation

The Decision-Maker's Guide to Equity Compensation

Corey Rosen
Pam Chernoff
Daniel N. Janich
Scott Rodrick

The National Center for Employee Ownership
Oakland, California

The Decision-Maker's Guide to Equity Compensation
Corey Rosen, Pam Chernoff, Daniel N. Janich, and Scott Rodrick

Book design by Scott Rodrick.

The National Center for Employee Ownership
1736 Franklin Street, 8th Floor
Oakland, CA 94612
(510) 208-1300
(510) 272-9510 (fax)
Web site: www.nceo.org

ISBN-10: 1-932924-38-8
ISBN-13: 978-1-932924-38-1

Contents

Preface

Providing employees with some kind of ownership or ownership right through equity compensation is a widespread practice in American business. There are many publications available detailing the legal, tax, accounting, and financial planning aspects of equity compensation, but, until now, none exclusively focused on helping people who are designing plans decide what kinds of equity to choose, and who should get how much and when. Are options a better fit than restricted stock? What are the pros and cons of phantom stock and stock appreciation rights? Should employees be able to buy stock? If so, how?

Aside from picking a form of equity, businesses must decide who will be eligible, what rules will govern how and when employees can get awards, how awards will be earned, what rights employees will have, how to provide liquidity for the awards, and many other critical issues. All too often, these decisions are made based on some rule of thumb ("10% is a good amount of equity to give out"), what someone has heard "everyone else" does, or what a consultant with limited experience advises (often what the consultant knows best, not necessarily what would work best).

Many technical issues have to be considered, such as the tax consequences of the plan, securities law rules, accounting issues, and contractual concerns. While these are important, plans should be primarily driven by corporate objectives for attracting, retaining, and motivating employees.

This book looks at these critical design issues, providing an easy way to compare different types of equity, think about different plan rules, and understand the key technical considerations in setting up and managing a plan. This book also includes a CD with a prerecorded Webinar (an audiovisual presentation viewed through a Web browser) by coauthor Corey Rosen on sharing equity with employees through stock options, restricted stock, phantom stock, stock appreciation rights, and other means. (See the appendix for more information.)

Writing this book was a team effort by Corey Rosen, Pam Chernoff (a Certified Equity Professional), and Scott Rodrick, all very experienced NCEO staff. In addition, Dan Janich of the Janich Law Group coauthored the chapter on securities law; Alisa Baker of Levine & Baker provided a technical review of the chapter on stock purchase plans; and Alan Nadel of Strategic Apex Group LLC carefully audited the accounting chapter. The NCEO's Christine Zwerling, also a Certified Equity Professional, added valuable input for several of the book's chapters. We very much thank these experts for their generous assistance. Any errors, of course, are ours.

NCEO members should feel free to call us to pursue any issues related to equity compensation in further detail. More technical material on all the subjects in this book can be found in other NCEO publications. Go to www.nceo.org for details.

Creating an Equity Compensation Plan That Works for Your Company

COREY ROSEN

In 2006, a national survey showed that 38% of the employees who worked for companies that have stock own at least some employer stock, or hold stock options or some other equity right. At the same time, equity compensation is making up larger and larger portions of executive pay, especially in larger companies. The growing importance of equity as an element of compensation is not surprising. Since the 1970s, inflation-adjusted wages have grown at less than 0.3% per year, while inflation-adjusted returns on equity during that time have been about 6% per year. So over the past 30 years, an investment in the market of $50,000 would be worth about $287,000, in real dollars, while an "investment" in wages of $50,000 would still be less than $60,000. This disparity is a historical anomaly. In the past, wages and return on capital have grown more or less in tandem. There are lots of explanations for this—globalization's downward pressure on wages, the economy's shift from manufacturing to service industries, "winner take all" compensation structures, and others—but the result is that more people want to get a piece of the equity pie.

At the same time, companies have put more emphasis on equity pay as their cultures shift from traditional, hierarchical management to leaner and more open participative approaches in which more employees at all levels are given increasing responsibilities to make more decisions (or at least to have input into more decisions) about more things more quickly. Traditional control mechanisms—threats, close supervision, individual incentive pay, highly structured and simplified tasks—are giving way to engagement models that rely more on employees' internal motivation. In effect, employees are being asked more and more to think and act like owners. In this environment, employees need a reason to care, and what better reason than to actually be owners?

Finally, employees are less loyal than they had been, in part because they believe employers are less loyal to them. An astonishing 75% of the respondents to a 2004 survey by the Society for Human Resource Management said they were looking for new jobs. The desire for better pay and better career opportunities, and unhappiness with their current jobs were (in that order) the main reasons. Even at the executive level, job tenure has become increasingly short, with average CEO tenure falling to about five years in public companies (comparable data are not available for private companies). Yet as employees have been given more responsibility, the costs of employee turnover have grown. When companies had mostly highly segmented, routine tasks, new employees could be trained quickly because there were so few things to learn. Now there is so much more to master, much of it company-specific, that even replacing line employees is very expensive, let alone key executives. A Mercer Human Resource Consulting study in 2005 found that 43% of respondents put the cost of training a new employee at $10,000; one-fifth put it at $30,000. Attracting and retaining good people, therefore, has become more essential than ever, yet also much harder. In an economy in which virtually every company proclaims "people are our most important asset," a company's actual treatment of employees may be the key differentiator between winners and losers.

Research on equity compensation plans indicates ownership can be a powerful tool in this effort. Turnover rates at companies with broad-based ownership plans are significantly lower than at companies without these plans. A study by WorldatWork found that, dollar-for-dollar, stock options were the most cost effective of several approaches to decreasing turnover. Research by the NCEO has shown that the more stock employees get in employee stock ownership plans (ESOPs), the less likely they are to leave. Turnover rates in 100% ESOP companies, in fact, are about half of that in comparable non-employee-owned companies. Employees also consistently report that, other things being equal, the more equity they have, the more they like their jobs regardless of whether the equity is in the form of options or in an ESOP.

There are many ways in which to share ownership with employees. These include stock options, restricted stock, restricted stock units (RSUs), and performance shares, all ways to provide employees with direct share ownership rights. Phantom stock is designed to give employees the equivalent value of ownership, but not actual shares. Stock appreciation rights (SARs) can be designed to pay out in either shares or cash. Tax-qualified employee stock purchase plans (ESPPs) and direct share purchase plans allow employees to purchase shares directly. And a form of retirement plan called an ESOP is funded by the company and provides ownership to most or all employees through a trust. How do you choose which one vehicle or combination of vehicles makes sense?

Cultural Concerns

Of course simply handing out equity is not a magic bullet. Effective ownership companies also create what we call "ownership cultures" by sharing information about company financial and substantive progress, providing structured opportunities for employees to have input into decisions affecting their work, and training them not just in their jobs but in how the company works. The NCEO has publications and other materials on creating such cultures; other NCEO publications provide in-depth looks at various kinds of plans and offer model plan documents. This book discusses the various forms of employee equity arrangements, including the basic tax, securities law, accounting, financial, and practical implications of each. We also discuss key issues in designing any kind of equity plan, such as who should get how much subject to what conditions.

Overview of Equity Alternatives

Subsequent chapters will explore the various forms of equity in more depth. It's useful, however, to start with an overview. The remainder of this chapter looks briefly at the kinds of equity programs available.

Basic Forms of Individual Equity Plans

There are five basic kinds of individual equity compensation awards: stock options, restricted stock, SARs, phantom stock, and direct stock awards. Many of these have variations as well. Each form provides employees with some special consideration in price or terms. We do not cover here simply offering employees the right to buy stock as any other investor would receive.

Stock options give employees the right to buy a number of shares at a price fixed at grant for a defined number of years into the future. As with other forms of stock awards described here, the right to exercise the award is usually available only after certain vesting requirements are met, most often working a certain number of years or meeting a performance target. *Restricted stock* gives employees the right to acquire shares by gift or purchase at fair market value or a discounted value. Employees can take possession of the shares, however, only once certain restrictions lapse, usually meaning once vesting restrictions are satisfied. *Phantom stock* pays a future cash or share bonus at a specified date equal to the value of a certain number of shares. *RSUs* are essentially phantom stock awards settled in the form of shares. *SARs* provide the right to the increase in the value of a designated number of shares, paid in cash or shares. Unlike phantom stock, SARs can be freely exercisable after vesting, although they sometimes pay out at a specific date or upon a specific occurrence. *Stock awards* are direct grants of shares to employees. In some cases, these shares are granted only if certain corporate, group, or individual performance conditions are met. These awards are usually called *performance shares*.

All of these individual equity award types can be provided to any employee on any terms the company chooses, with some very limited exceptions. Companies can make decisions about who gets the awards, how much they get (with some limits for one kind of stock option), how the company will make a market for the shares, and, within some limits, terms and conditions for the award (such as vesting and how long the award can be exercised). Generally, awards are taxable to the employee as ordinary income when the employee has a nonforfeitable right to them; the employer then gets a corresponding deduction. One kind of stock option, called an incentive stock option, allows an employee the possibility of paying only capital gains taxes on the award, but in that case, the company does not get a deduction.

Stock Purchase Plans

Employees can purchase shares directly or through a specialized kind of plan for this purpose called an employee stock purchase plan (ESPP). When employees simply purchase shares directly, they use their after-tax dollars to do so. In some cases, the employer may make loans to the employee to buy the stock. Under the Sarbanes-Oxley Act of 2002 companies are not allowed to make loans to company insiders; however, they can provide loans to other employees. To avoid tax and securities problems, the loans should be recourse notes with an interest rate at or above the applicable federal rate. Companies can choose which employees can buy stock, based on whatever criterion they choose.

Many ESPPs, by contrast, are designed to meet the requirements of Section 423 of the Internal Revenue Code (for simplicity, in this chapter we will refer to plans that comply with Section 423 as ESPPs and to those that don't as direct stock purchase plans). Under that tax code section, the plan must be available at least to all full-time employees except for those who would, after the ESPP grant, own 5% or more of the company; they must be excluded. However, the company can restrict participation to those who have been employed for at least two years and/or those who work more than 20 hours per week or more than five months per year. The plan must be offered on the same basis to all employees who participate, and no employee can acquire more than $25,000 in stock in one year, based on the stock's fair market value on the first day of the offering period. Employees typically agree to have some of their after-tax pay reserved to save toward purchasing shares during an "offering period" that can be a few months to a few years. Companies can (but are not required to) allow employees to buy stock at either the lower price at the beginning or end of the offering period and at up to a 15% discount off the stock's fair market value on the date when the purchase price is set. If the stock price is $10 at the start of the offering period when the employee begins to set payroll aside, and the employee buys stock at the end of, say, a six-month offering period when it is worth $12, he or she might be able to buy it for as little as $8.50 (i.e., 15% off the $10 price from the beginning of the offering period); if it drops to $6 at the end of six months, the employee could buy for $5.10 (i.e., 15% off the $6 price at the end of the offering period). If certain requirements are met, the employee can usually receive better tax treatment than with a nonqualified ESPP.

Any kind of stock purchase plan must comply with state and federal securities laws. These laws generally provide exemptions from stock registration requirements for offers to employees meeting certain rules, rules almost every closely held company can meet without compromising what it wants to do with the plan. But all plans offered broadly to employees must provide for detailed financial disclosure and investment risk discussion. Moreover, if companies end up with 500 or more shareholders (a number that currently includes option holders[1] unless the company has received an exemption letter for option holders from the SEC), they can become *de facto* public companies. For these reasons, ESPPs are primarily, albeit not exclusively, found in public companies.

ESOPs, 401(k) Plans, and Profit Sharing Plans

ESOPs, 401(k) plans, and tax-qualified profit sharing plans are all covered by the Employee Retirement Income Security Act (ERISA). All provide means for employees to accumulate assets on a tax-fa-

---

1.   As of mid-2007, the SEC had proposed excluding option holders from this number if certain conditions are met.

vored basis over the term of their employment. Employers get tax deductions for their contributions to these plans, and employees don't pay taxes on the money they or their employers contribute to their accounts until they withdraw the money. All of these plans operate through trusts overseen by plan fiduciaries charged with operating them in the best interests of plan participants, and they all are subject to a variety of rules to assure that the benefits of the plan are provided to all qualified employees and on a basis that does not discriminate against lower-level employees. While benefits in the plan can be based on relative compensation (within limits) or on how much employees choose to defer, all employees with at least 1,000 hours of service in a year must be eligible to participate in the plan, and their benefits must be vested over not more than three to six years, depending on the plan and how vesting occurs.

More than 9,000 companies provide ownership to employees through ESOPs, a very specific creature of U.S. tax law with very specific rules and benefits. Unfortunately, this term is often incorrectly used to refer in a generic sense to any kind of ownership plan. Sometimes a stock option plan will be called an "ESOP" as though it were an acronym for "employee stock option plan" instead of for "employee stock ownership plan." (Other countries sometimes use the term in different contexts—for example, "employee share option plans" in India are referred to as ESOPs, but are not the same as U.S. ESOPs.)

Almost all U.S. ESOPs are found in closely held companies. They are generally entirely funded by the employer. They provide a variety of tax benefits to everyone involved. In addition to the employer's ability to deduct contributions to the plan, the business owners who sell their stock to the ESOP can in some circumstances defer taxation on the money they receive from the sale. S corporations that have ESOPs avoid taxes on profits attributable to the ESOP's share of ownership. As a result, S corporations that are 100% owned by their ESOPs do not pay federal income taxes. C corporations can deduct from their taxes both the principal and the interest on any loans their ESOPs had to procure to pay for the shares.

Although ESOPs are most commonly used to provide a market for the shares of a selling owner in a closely held corporation, they can also be used to finance growth or just to provide employees with an ownership interest in the company. They cannot, however, be set up in LLCs or partnerships because they must own employer stock, not some equivalent.

Employers that want to offer company stock in tax-qualified retirement plans can also use 401(k) plans and profit sharing plans as vehicles for employee ownership. Companies can simply make their contributions to the plans in the form of shares, provided they can establish a fair market value for the stock (such as by having an appraisal or being publicly traded), but in 401(k) plans they must allow employees to diversify out of company stock after they've held it for three years. Employees can also buy company stock in a 401(k) plan, subject to securities law requirements that may make this difficult in closely held companies. They cannot, however, be forced to hold company stock in their 401(k) accounts. This book discusses ESOPs in more detail than 401(k) or profit sharing plans, because ESOPs are clearly the most tax-favored and effective means to use an ERISA-qualified plan to share ownership broadly.

Kinds of Equity

Companies can offer employees a variety of kinds of equity in their plans, with some restrictions. ESOPs, for instance, must own stock with the highest combination of voting and dividend rights (typically Class A common) or stock that is convertible into that class of stock. Profit sharing and 401(k) plans cannot own options or other forms of equity rights. The necessity that the ESOP get shares that carry voting rights (or shares convertible into such shares) is, as we will see later, not really a problem and should not be a factor in choosing or not choosing an ESOP as it does not mean that owners who want to maintain control of the company must cede that control to workers.

There is no such voting rights requirement for stock option, restricted stock, performance share, or stock purchase plans. Although they all typically provide the right to buy or own common stock, they could just as well offer preferred shares or some other variety of common stock. (Preferred and super common stock typically have higher dividend and/or liquidation rights; in a few cases, special classes of common with special voting rights have been created.) The shares may or may not have voting rights, although the existence or lack of these rights may affect how the shares are valued. A company that does not have stock because it is an LLC or a partnership, for example, can offer ownership by granting partnership rights or units instead of stock.

The issue of whether unvested or unexercised equity awards can pay dividends is specific to each type of vehicle and thus is discussed in the individual chapters. In some cases, dividends paid on such awards lead to steep taxes for the award recipient under the tax rules governing deferred compensation.

Making the Decision

The chapter on designing equity plans will help readers think through the various issues involved in choosing a plan or plans and deciding on their features. Before thinking through the nitty-gritty of plan details, however, spend some time thinking about what the plan is for. Is it for business transition? Is it to reward all employees or just some? Is it to motivate employee behavior, and if so, is it aimed at some people or everyone? What kind of ownership rights are you prepared to share (plans can be designed to provide almost none, some, or all of the rights)? Do you want ownership to be a right of employment, or should there be hurdles to getting it? Does it matter to you whether employees actually become shareholders or is your primary concern that they be rewarded for gains in the company's share price?

Table I-1 looks at the various reasons why a company might set up an employee-ownership plan on the column side of the table and the attributes of plans owners may want on the row side. You can use it as a guide to help think through some of the key issues in picking a plan.

After learning about the basics of equity plans, the next step should be to talk to other businesses about their experiences with sharing ownership. If you do not know any companies that share ownership, you can go to a conference where companies with vari-

Table I-1. Characteristics of Employee Ownership Plans

	Incentive for selected employees only	Incentive for all employees	Raising capital	Generate corporate tax savings*
Retain management control	Any individual equity award Subsidized stock purchase plans	ESOPs, 401(k), profit sharing plans Broadly granted equity awards ESPPs	Direct stock purchase plans, ESPPs	ESOPs, 401(k), profit sharing plans
Base awards on merits or other individual criteria	Any individual equity awards Subsidized stock purchase plans	Any individual equity awards Subsidized stock purchase plans	Subsidized or unsubsidized stock purchase plans	None
Employees must be willing to put up their own money	Subsidized or unsubsidized stock purchase plans Restricted stock plans requiring share purchase ESPPs	ESPPs	ESPPs Subsidized or unsubsidized stock purchase plans	None
Simplicity	Phantom stock, SARs	Subsidized or unsubsidized stock purchase plans	Subsidized or unsubsidized stock purchase plans	None
Do not issue actual shares	Phantom stock, cash-settled SARs	Phantom stock, cash-settled SARs	None	None
Provide ownership transition	Any kind of stock purchase plan	ESOPs or direct stock purchase plans available to all employees	Any kind of direct stock purchase plan	ESOPs

*Employers can deduct equity compensation benefits paid to employees except for incentive stock options and tax-qualified ESPPs (but even with these two plans, the company is eligible for a deduction if the employee fails to meet the holding period requirements for capital gains treatment). Here, we focus only on plans that generate tax savings beyond those normally available for the payment of compensation.

ous sorts of plans, from ESOPs to options, are represented (such as the NCEO's annual conference) or, if you are an NCEO member, call us for suggestions. Finally, when you are ready to proceed, make sure you find qualified professional advisors who actually have set up many of the specific kinds of plans you choose.

In other words, make this decision as seriously as you would any other essential strategic decision, such as selling the company, making an acquisition, or going into a new line of business. Ownership is a powerful tool that can work very well or very badly. It needs to be carefully thought through.

The Plan of This Book

The following chapters look at several key issues:

- Considerations in choosing and designing any equity plan
- Stock options
- Stock grants, stock purchase arrangements, restricted stock, and restricted stock units
- Phantom stock and stock appreciation rights (SARs)
- ESOPs, profit sharing, and 401(k) plans
- Deferred compensation rules
- Accounting issues
- Securities law considerations
- Special considerations for public companies
- Designing an equity incentive plan
- Issues in providing equity compensation to executives

In chapters on specific forms of equity compensation, we discuss their tax and legal implications and look at plan design alternatives.

We hope you find the book useful. It draws on more than 25 years of experience at the National Center for Employee Ownership. We can always learn from your comments, however, and warmly invite them.

CHAPTER 1

Stock Options

COREY ROSEN

Stock options are still the most popular form of equity compensation. Part of that stems from the fact that until 2006, companies did not have to show any charge to earnings on their income statements for stock options that had fixed terms, vested over time, and had set exercise prices at grant. Other forms of equity compensation, including performance-vested options, did require a charge to earnings. While this was simply an accounting procedure—it did not affect the company's taxes or its cash flow—it did provide better "optics" for investors, making companies' income statements look better than they might have otherwise. Now almost all forms of equity compensation require a charge to earnings, and other approaches are gaining traction, but options, partly because of their familiarity, remain the most common equity strategy.

Stock options provide an employee (or other service provider) the right to purchase shares at a specified price for a set number of years into the future. When an employee exercises the option, the company must make that number of shares available, either by buying them from existing owners or issuing shares. This chapter explores the different kinds of stock options, how they work, how they are taxed, and what you should think about in deciding whether to grant options or other forms of equity compensation.

How Options Work

Basics

A few key concepts help explain how stock options work:

- *Option:* A contract between a company and an employee grant-ing the employee the right to buy a specific number of the company's shares at a fixed price within a certain period of time.

- *Exercise:* The purchase of stock pursuant to an option.

- *Exercise price:* The price at which the stock can be purchased. This is also called the "strike price" or "grant price." In most plans, the exercise price is the current fair market value of the stock at the time the grant is made.

- *Spread:* The difference between the exercise price and the market value of the stock.

- *Option term:* The length of time the employee can hold the op-tion before it expires.

- *Vesting:* The requirement that must be met in order to have the right to exercise the option—usually continuation of service for a specific period of time or the meeting of a performance goal.

A company grants an employee options to buy a stated number of shares at a defined grant price. The options vest over a period of time or once certain individual, group, or corporate goals are met. Some companies set time-based vesting schedules, but allow options to vest sooner if performance goals are met. Once vested, the employee can exercise the option at the exercise price at any time over the option term up to the expiration date. For instance, an employee might be granted the right to buy 1,000 shares at $10 per share. The options vest 25% per year over four years and have a term of 10 years. If the stock price goes up, the employee will pay $10 per share to buy the stock. If it goes down, the employee will not be able to exercise the options. If the stock goes to $25 after seven years, and the employee exercises all options, the spread between the exercise price and the exercise date fair market value is $15 per share.

Kinds of Options

Options are either incentive stock options (ISOs) or nonqualified stock options (NSOs), which are sometimes referred to as nonstatutory stock options. When an employee exercises an NSO, the spread on exercise is taxable to the employee as ordinary income, even if the shares are not yet sold. The company can deduct a corresponding amount. There is no legally required holding period for the shares after exercise, although the company may impose one. Any subsequent gain or loss on the shares after exercise is taxed as a capital gain or treated as a capital loss when the optionee sells the shares. The gain or loss is long-term if the shares have been held for more than a year, or short-term if they have been held for a year or less.

An ISO enables an employee to: (1) defer taxation on the option from the date of exercise until the date of sale of the underlying shares, and (2) pay taxes at capital gains rates, rather than ordinary income tax rates, if certain conditions are met:

1. The employee must hold the stock for at least one year after the exercise date and for two years after the grant date.

2. Only $100,000 worth of stock can first become exercisable in any calendar year. This is measured by the stock's fair market value on the options' grant date. It means that only $100,000 in grant price value can become eligible to be exercised in any one year. If there is overlapping vesting, such as would occur if ISOs are granted annually and vest gradually, companies must track outstanding ISOs to ensure the amounts that become vested under different grants will not exceed $100,000 in value in any one year. Any portion of an ISO grant that exceeds the limit is treated as an NSO.

3. The exercise price must not be less than the fair market value of the company's stock on the date of the grant. IRS guidelines

must be followed to assure that the value set for the shares is fair market value.

4. ISOs can be granted only to employees.

5. The option must be granted pursuant to a written plan that must be approved by shareholders within 12 months before or after the board of directors adopts it. The plan must specify how many shares can be issued under it and identify the class of employees eligible to receive grants.

6. Options must be granted within 10 years of the plan's adoption by the board of directors, and each option must be exercised within 10 years of its grant date.

7. If, on the grant date, an employee owns more than 10% of the voting power of all outstanding stock of the company, the ISO exercise price must be at least 110% of the fair market value of the stock on that date and the option may not be exercisable for more than five years.

If all the rules for ISOs are met, then the eventual sale of the shares is called a "qualifying disposition," and the employee pays long-term capital gains tax on the total increase in value between the grant price and sale price. The company does not receive a tax deduction for a qualifying disposition.

A sale before the holding period has elapsed is called a "disqualifying disposition" because it disqualifies the option from favorable tax treatment. In that case, the option recipient must pay ordinary income taxes on the lesser of the spread between the exercise price and the exercise date fair market value or the spread between the exercise price and the sale price. If the stock price rises between the exercise date and the sale date, then the difference between the stock's prices on those two dates is taxed at capital gains rates. If the stock is sold at a loss, no taxes are due.[1] Both the ordinary income tax and capital gains taxes must be reflected on the employee's tax return for the year in which the stock is sold.

---

1. An exception to this exists in situations such as a disposition by way of gift where a loss would not be recognized. In such cases, the sale of shares at a loss is treated as a capital loss.

An employee who exercises an ISO but does not sell the shares in the year of exercise does, however, face a possible alternative minimum tax (AMT) liability. The spread on the option at exercise is a "preference item" for purposes of the AMT. So even though the shares may not have been sold, the exercise means the employee must add back the gain on exercise, along with other AMT preference items, to see whether an AMT payment is due. Employees can avoid the AMT liability by selling their shares in the calendar year in which they exercise, although this disqualifies the ISO and subjects the spread on exercise to ordinary income tax. An alternative strategy is to sell enough stock to cover the projected AMT, then hold onto the remaining shares long enough to meet the ISO holding period. The worst-case scenario is when an employee exercises an ISO in one year, then sells the shares in the next, but before satisfying the holding period requirement. In that case, both AMT and income tax are triggered.

Private companies need to consider the AMT issue carefully before issuing ISOs. Employees who exercise their options will often face an AMT obligation but, lacking a market to sell shares, not have the cash to pay the tax. If the company's value declines, they could end up paying the AMT on gains they can never realize.

The company does not take a tax deduction when there is a qualifying disposition. If, however, there is a disqualifying disposition, most often because the employee exercises and sells before meeting the required holding periods, the company can claim a tax deduction in the amount the employee must claim as ordinary income.

Deferred Compensation Issues and Stock Valuation

ISOs are not subject to the deferred compensation rules connected to Internal Revenue Code Section 409A, nor are NSOs if they are issued at fair market value. It is essential that companies comply with the new rules for setting fair market value for option grants to ensure that the awards are made at a price the IRS will consider to be an accurate value. This book's chapter on deferred compensation discusses this issue in detail. The bottom line for option holders is that awards the IRS considers to have been granted at a discount will result in the option being subject to Section 409A. If the discounted option grant does not comply with the Section 409A requirements, then the recipient will be assessed a 20% penalty plus interest in addition to regular income taxes at the time the option vests.

For publicly traded companies, 409A allows the use of any reasonable method for deriving fair market value from stock market transactions, including the last sale price before grant, first sale price after grant, closing price on the trading day before or after grant, or using an average price over a period of up to 30 days before or after the grant as long as an irrevocable commitment to grant the right is made before the averaging period begins.

For privately held companies, the final regulations do not mandate the use of an independent appraiser; however, the person charged with determining the fair market value must have sufficient knowledge, experience, training, or education to be qualified to do the appraisal. The NCEO strongly recommends using an independent appraiser to shift the burden of proof from the granting company to the IRS if the valuation is challenged. In the past, many privately held companies picked a number for the share price that seemed "right," or used a number from an old valuation or other seemingly reasonable source without putting much thought into the process. None of these approaches will be sufficient now. While the rules allow for any reasonable method of valuation, a formal appraisal is not only safer but provides a more precise assessment of just how much value the company is sharing.

Exercising an Option

There are several ways to exercise a stock option: by using cash to purchase the shares, by exchanging shares the optionee already owns (often called a stock swap), by working with a stock broker to do a same-day sale, or by executing a sell-to-cover transaction (these latter two are often called cashless exercises, although that term actually includes stock swaps and a few other forms of exercise as well). Any one stock option plan may provide for just one or two of these alternatives or may allow many of them. Private companies frequently restrict the exercise or sale of the shares acquired through exercise until the company is sold or goes public, so same-day sale or sell-to-cover transactions are typically excluded from private company plans or restricted until after the company goes public.

The most common form of exercise of an option in a closely held company is simply for the employee to pay cash for the shares. If the options are NSOs, the employer will also have to withhold the taxes the employee owes upon exercise. Many employers allow employees to use some of the option shares to pay for this obligation, but the company must ensure it has enough cash available to submit to the tax authorities.

In a same-day sale, the employee works with a stock broker, usually a "captive broker" designated by the company. The optionee notifies the company and the stock broker of the desire to exercise, the company provides the broker with confirmation that the employee has exercisable options, and the broker sells the shares. From the sale proceeds, the broker delivers the option price plus any withholding taxes to the company and delivers the remaining proceeds, minus any broker commissions, to the employee. Although called a "same-day" sale, the settlement process can take up to three days after the sale date.

A sell-to-cover exercise is a combination of cash and same-day sale exercises. The stock broker does a same-day sale to come up with enough money to cover the exercise and withholding taxes plus the funds required to do a cash exercise of additional shares, allowing the employee to become a shareholder without having to put out any cash of his or her own.

In a stock swap, the employee simply exchanges shares he or she already owns for the option shares. For instance, if the employee has the right to exercise options for 1,000 shares at $10 each, and the current share price is $25, the employee would exchange 400 shares to exercise those 1,000 options. That's because the 400 shares the employee owns are worth $10,000, which is the amount needed to cover the exercise price. The employee would come out of the transaction owning 1,000 shares, instead of just 400 shares. However, if taxes are due, then the employee might choose to turn in enough shares to cover the taxes as well, if the plan allows it. Stock swaps are more commonly used with ISOs where taxes do not have to be paid at the time of exercise. However, if the already owned shares used to effect the swap are ISO shares that have not been held for the statutory holding period, the swap is a disqualifying disposition of those shares.

Where the Shares Come From

Companies can settle option transactions by either issuing new shares or buying them back from existing shareholders. Issuing new shares is dilutive in terms of the percentage of ownership held by existing owners; buying back shares is anti-dilutive, but is a non-deductible expense that reduces the overall value of the company. Public companies tend to buy back shares if they have extra cash and believe their stock is a good value. Closely held companies, having less opportunity to buy back shares, usually just issue additional shares.

Accounting

Accounting rules for equity compensation plans that became effective in 2006 require companies to use an option-pricing model to calculate the present value of all option awards as of the date of grant and show this as an expense on their income statements. The expense should be adjusted based on vesting experience (so shares that will never vest do not count as a charge to compensation). The accounting chapter of this book discusses stock option accounting in more detail.

Securities Law Issues

Another chapter of this book looks at securities issues in detail. In brief, however, stock options are subject to securities law considerations. For public companies, options must comply with insider trading rules, reporting rules, short-swing profit rules, rules regarding resale of securities after an IPO, and other requirements of being a public company. Currently, holders of options count toward the 500-shareholder rule that, along with having $10 million or more in assets, determines whether a company is a de facto public company, even if its stock is not traded on an exchange. However, as of mid-2007, the Securities and Exchange Commission was considering a change that would exclude the holders of stock options from this number. The SEC has been willing to grant exemptions from this requirement for most standard option plans, but companies must specifically request one. Public companies must register their option grants in a simplified filing, Form S-8. Public companies must also make detailed disclosures about options, along with other equity awards, for top executives under 2006 executive compensation disclosure rules.

Securities registration is a bigger issue for closely held companies. A number of exemptions are available; the most commonly used is Rule 701 under the Securities Act of 1933. Rule 701 allows companies to offer unregistered securities to employees and other service providers under a written compensation agreement as long as the amount sold in a 12-month period does not exceed the greater of: (1) $1 million; (2) 15% of the issuer's total assets; or (3) 15% of the outstanding securities of that class. Other limited exemptions from registration are available as well. However, even if an exemption is available, companies must comply with anti-fraud rules requiring them to provide certain financial information to option holders.

Should You Use Options or Something Else?

How They Reward

Even with a level accounting playing field, options are still appealing to many companies and investors who like the idea that employees are rewarded only if the share price goes up. From an employee standpoint, options are especially enticing in growth-oriented companies. Analysts often say that options are a highly leveraged award. What they mean by this is that the value of each option grant can go up very quickly relative to its grant value. If my employer outright gives me one share of stock worth $100 on the grant date, and I sell it five years later for $150, I am $150 richer. If the stock drops to $50, I am still $50 in the clear since I invested nothing. However, if my company decides to grant me an option award, I will probably ask for the right to buy more than one share at $100. In many companies, that works out to about three options for each actual share granted. To understand this, ask yourself how much you would pay today for the right to buy three shares of a company's stock at $100 per share any time between four years from now and 10 years from now. You obviously would pay a lot less than $100 because the stock price could go down, in which case that right to purchase shares would be worthless.

So say you get three options at $100 per share and the price goes to $150 five years later, as in the example above. If you exercise the options and sell the shares, your return is 3 x $50, or $150, a 50% return. On the other hand, if the stock goes down, unlike in the example above, your option is worthless. So options leverage future growth at a much higher multiple than do straight grants. Whether that is good or bad for your investors and for your employees depends on your growth prospects. That is why some mature companies have switched to restricted stock, a kind of full-value stock grant, instead of options. At the other extreme, if your company is just getting started and its stock value is very low anyway, options don't have much downside risk. Most companies are somewhere in the middle and must figure out how to make the choice between these two approaches, or decide how to provide some of one and some of the other.

Dilution

When options are accounted for, each option is worth only some fraction of a full-value share grant. But when investors measure dilution from the issuance of equity awards, options count exactly the same as share grants. Although options are not included in the calculation of regular earnings per share, all outstanding options—even unvested options—are included in the number of shares outstanding in calculating diluted earnings per share. However, the company is allowed to subtract the number of shares it would be able to buy back with the exercise proceeds if all options were exercised. Options appear more dilutive than they are in an economic sense compared to share grants. For instance, if a company has to issue three options to provide the same economic value at grant as one actual share, the dilution from the options appears to be three times as great, but the economic cost to the company at grant is, by definition, the same because the option grant number has been specifically calibrated to be equal to the same ultimate cash cost to the company as the stock grant.

This matters much more to public companies, of course, which worry about investor perceptions. Closely held companies are in a much better position to explain these issues to investors.

Complexity

Options are somewhat more complex than their closest equivalent, stock appreciation rights (SARs), which pay holders the appreciation in the share price between the grant date and exercise or payout date. The main difference between the two is that while the recipient of a stock option must pay money to the company to exercise the option, the exercise of a SAR occurs at no cost to the recipient. And unlike stock options, SARs cannot be structured as a tax-qualified form of equity compensation.

Familiarity

One important advantage of choosing options is that they are familiar to employees. Some employees may be more suspicious of phantom stock or SARs. Restricted stock is more intuitively understandable, but, in some situations, employees may not understand that getting one or two shares of restricted stock is as good as getting three option shares. These problems can be overcome with enough communication, but companies need to commit to that effort.

Deciding on Option Rules

The introduction to this book discusses how to decide who gets how much equity under what conditions. In addition to the issues raised there, which apply to all kinds of equity awards, there are two specific considerations for options that deserve special attention.

Vesting

Performance-vested awards are a favorite of equity compensation consultants and shareholders, who like the way this requirement means the options deliver no value unless certain corporate, group, or individual goals are met. A key consideration is whether the award should vest upon achievement of a target or be granted that way (or both). Awards that are granted based on performance provide a more immediate reward for group or individual behaviors; performance vesting makes the occasion of the grant less motivating, but it may be linked to working to achieve a goal more. Time vesting obviously rewards tenure, something most companies want to encourage and that may seem more certain to employees than meeting performance goals. Employees may discount the value of the option grant less as a result. Some closely held companies do not allow vesting until a liquidity event. Pros and cons of this are discussed below.

Exercise

Some closely held companies grant options that will not vest, and thus become exercisable, until the company is sold or goes public. For a company that has a clear plan to do that within the next few years, this makes sense, assuming employees know that the company is planning such a liquidity event. After all, it normally is unsettling to employees to know that in a few years the company may be sold. They naturally worry that their jobs will disappear. But assuming employees understand and accept this uncertainty, vesting upon a liquidity event helps preserve needed cash while still providing employees with both an incentive to remain with the company and a promise of a reward that seems reasonably close at hand. On the other hand, if the company even might stay private for more than few years, grants that will not vest if there is no sale or IPO can cause problems. Employees tend to undervalue future benefits, and the more uncertain they seem, the less they value them. That means you'll have to give away more options to get the same incentive. Moreover, some people you want to motivate may not think they are likely to stay this indefinite period of time, in which case the option awards do nothing to motivate them—even though, in fact, they may end up being there when the liquidity event occurs. It is worth considering, then, providing vesting after some period of time, such as four or five years, perhaps with an option to sell the shares back to the company once exercised. It is also possible to provide for vesting after a certain amount of time has elapsed or upon a sale or IPO, whichever comes first.

Closely held companies that allow exercise before a liquidity event face the issue of how employees will come up with the assets to exercise their options. Generally, employees need to pay cash, because they probably do not have existing shares to trade. A cashless exercise of an option makes the option identical to a stock appreciation right, discussed in a later chapter (because the employee ends up with the net cash from the gain on the shares, minus taxes, much like a cash-settled stock appreciation right). If a cashless exercise is used for options, the company might as well grant stock appreciation rights and avoid the extra complexity. This may also mean the company doesn't have to issue as many shares to award recipients.

Employees who are required to pay cash to exercise NSOs will also have to produce enough cash to cover the taxes on the exercise, but will have no cash from stock sale proceeds to deal with them. With ISOs, the employee may have AMT obligations upon exercise. Companies can handle the cash needs by paying a special bonus, but that itself is taxable. Companies could settle the option exercise in shares net of taxes, however, although that still leaves the issue of where the employee gets the cash to exercise in the first place.

Conclusion

Options remain as popular as they are for good reasons. They are not right for every company, however. Just because most other people use options does not mean options are the right approach for your company.

For those wanting to explore the technical issues surrounding options in detail, we recommend the NCEO's publication *The Stock Options Book*.

CHAPTER 2

Unrestricted Stock Grants and Stock Purchase Plans

SCOTT RODRICK

This chapter discusses outright, unrestricted grants or sales of stock to employees. "Unrestricted" in this context means only that the grant is not subject to forfeiture if certain restrictions are not met. A separate chapter discusses what are formally called "restricted stock" arrangements, i.e., stock awards or sales that are granted subject to restrictions, such as performance or vesting criteria, and are subject to forfeiture if those criteria are not met. (Also do not confuse this meaning of "restricted" with references to shares that are "restricted securities" in that they have not been registered under the Securities Act of 1933 and/or have restrictions placed on them, such as a requirement that they be sold back to the company.)

For many people, outright grants or sales to employees seem the most natural thing to do when establishing an employee stock plan. However, as noted below, individual grants or sales to employees bring complications with them. And although formal employee stock purchase plans (ESPPs) for a company's workers are very common in the U.S., they are found almost solely in public companies. This chapter discusses direct stock grants, stock sales, and stock purchase plans, and then addresses special liquidity, valuation, and securities issues that closely held companies face when implementing plans like these.

Direct Stock Grants (Stock Bonuses)

Conceptually speaking, perhaps the simplest form of equity compensation is a direct, unrestricted stock grant to an individual employee. These are often called "stock bonus" programs, a term that, like "restricted stock," can have more than one meaning. The other meaning of "stock bonus" is the stock bonus plan, a defined contribution retirement plan (akin to a 401(k) plan) that covers a broad group of employees and provides benefits in the form of company stock. This section discusses stock bonuses in the first sense, i.e., shares of company stock given to individual employees.

Structure and Use of Direct Stock Grants

Direct stock grants are straightforward and, unlike stock plans that are tax-qualified under the Internal Revenue Code (the Code), such as Section 423 ESPPs, discussed later in this chapter, or employee stock ownership plans (ESOPs), discussed later in this book, they have no particular legal requirements or restrictions on their use. The company can give them to a single person, to a group or groups, or to all employees. Direct stock grants can be used in a variety of ways as the company pleases. For example, a grant can be given as a bonus, as an adjunct to other stock arrangements (such as giving employees a free share of stock for every share they buy through a stock purchase program), or even as part of the salary at a cash-starved startup company.

The shares that are granted may be "restricted" in the sense of transferability restrictions, such as that the shares can be resold only to the company; that they must be resold to the company when employment terminates; or that the company has a right of first refusal when the shares are sold. This allows a private company to keep stock "in the family" (literally or figuratively) and avoid ex-employers or unwanted outsiders gaining ownership and perhaps some degree of control.

Since a direct stock grant makes the employee a shareholder, that person now will have the same voting rights and other privileges as do other shareholders of that class of securities. For a given employee, employee group, or everyone receiving stock grants, the company may wish to use shares with certain voting attributes or even create a new class of shares with the desired attributes. Even in S corporations, which are limited to one class of stock, it is permissible to have "differences in voting rights among the shares of common stock."[1] Typically, a company would limit the voting rights granted to employees because it was sensitive to control issues. However, the experience of many employee ownership companies, such as ESOP companies (which must pass through at least a minimum subset of voting rights to ESOP participants), is that this is not a big issue. Employees generally have no desire to use their voting rights to turn the company upside down and, in any event, would typically not own enough stock to do so. Also, excessively limiting voting rights may send the wrong message to employees: "We want you to think and work like an owner, but we don't trust you."

Aside from voting, rights, the company should consider what other rights the shares will have. Will they pay dividends, and if so, at what rate? Will the stock have special preferences in liquidation? Will it have "tag-along rights" that ensure that minority shareholders receive the same price as majority shareholders if the company is sold? Note that the presence and nature of these rights may affect not only the long-term financial benefits of the shares but also the fair market value of the shares at grant.

Coupling the Stock Grant with a Cash Bonus or Loan to Finance the Tax Obligation

As discussed below, the employee is subject to tax when the shares are awarded. Since the employee may keep the shares for some time, this means that as a practical matter, the employee may need money to pay the tax. Also, the company may wish to help finance the tax bill in one way or another in order to make the stock grant more of an incentive and less of a burden.

One way for the company to help finance an employee's tax bill is to couple the stock grant with a cash bonus. It is important to remember that this cash bonus is itself taxed (as noted below).

---

1. Code Section 1361(c)(4).

Alternatively, the company may loan employees the money to pay tax and provide for repayment by making deductions from subsequent paychecks. However, loans to directors and executive officers in public companies are illegal under Section 402 of the Sarbanes-Oxley Act of 2002. (Rule 3b-7 under the Securities Exchange Act of 1934 broadly defines "executive officers" as including any officer or other person who performs a policy-making function.) Although Sarbanes-Oxley does not apply to private companies, in some situations it may be viewed as setting the standard for corporate behavior in the matters it covers, for example in an ESOP-owned company (where the managers and directors are accountable to a broad group of owners[2]) or if the company plans to go public and thus soon will be subject to Sarbanes-Oxley. In such settings, a private company may be influenced by Sarbanes-Oxley when deciding whether and how to make loans to directors and executives.

Aside from Sarbanes-Oxley considerations, the "imputed interest" rules under Code Section 7872 also raise possible issues for loans. The imputed interest rules are complicated, but they generally provide that certain below-market-rate loans, including those between an employer and an employee (or between a company and a shareholder), are treated as if the discount from the market rate had been transferred from the lender to the borrower, and retransferred by the borrower to the lender as interest. This means that the forgone interest is treated as compensation paid to the employee and is taxed. (Similarly, the corporation is taxed as well.) For employer-employee loans, however, there is a de minimis exception where the aggregate outstanding amount of loans between the borrower and lender does not exceed $10,000, so long as a principal purpose of the loan is not to avoid federal taxation.[3] Given the complexity of the rules and the possible taxes involved, loans to employees should be carefully structured with the imputed interest rules (including all the details that are not discussed here) in mind.

---

2.   See Helen Morrison, Colleen Helmer, and Michael Falk, "Don't Be Fooled: Sarbanes-Oxley Applies to Private ESOP Companies," in *ESOPs and Corporate Governance*, 2nd ed. (Oakland, CA: NCEO, 2007).

3.   Code Section 7872(c)(3).

In deciding whether or how to help finance the tax obligations of employees who receive stock grants, the company may wish to consider the situations of various employee groups and treat different employees differently. For example, a wealthy executive may have no need for financing, whereas a rank-and-file worker with little or no savings may be a good candidate for a cash bonus to provide money for tax payments. (Of course, that wealthy executive may plead that he or she is a more important employee—or that his or her tax burden is much greater—and is thus more deserving of financial help for the tax obligation.) The company also may consider how long employees will have to wait to sell the shares, which might vary among employees depending on how the company structures the various grants. For example, if there is no market for the shares, the shares have transferability restrictions, and the company will not buy the shares back for some time, the employee essentially has no way of disposing of shares to raise money for the tax bill. On the other hand, if the company freely offers to buy back shares at any time, the employee can always sell some shares to pay the tax bill and thus is less in need of help to finance his or her tax obligations.

The company should consider the purpose of the stock grant (to motivate employees and align their interests with the company's, etc.) and make sure that its policies on helping finance the tax obligation do not conflict with that purpose. For example, someone who receives a stock grant and is hit by a tax bill they cannot pay is not going to be very motivated.

Tax and Accounting Treatment of Direct Stock Grants

Employee Considerations

As with a cash bonus, an employee given a direct stock grant recognizes (i.e., must reflect on his or her tax return) ordinary income for tax purposes when the grant is awarded and received. The amount of income is the value of the grant, i.e., the number of shares multiplied by the fair market value per share. Thus, if the grant is worth $10,000 and the employee has a combined federal and state tax rate of 30%, the employee recognizes $10,000 of ordinary income and will pay $3,000 in taxes. (In contrast, with a restricted stock grant—for example, a stock grant subject to vesting—income is not recognized until the restrictions lapse and the grant is no longer subject to a substantial risk of forfeiture. In this example, that would be when the restricted stock vests unless a Section 83(b) election were made. See the chapter on restricted stock for details.) Note that in some states (e.g., Delaware), the employee may need to pay a nominal amount—"par value"— for the shares to make the transfer effective even when it is a direct stock grant.

If the stock grant is coupled with a cash bonus (i.e., to pay the taxes on the stock grant), that cash bonus itself is taxed as well, of course. In the example in the above paragraph, if the company gives the employee a $3,000 cash bonus to fund the tax bill on the stock grant, the employee will in turn owe $900 ($3,000 taxed at the 30% rate in our example) on the cash bonus. In some cases, the company may also wish to make the employee whole with respect to the amount of taxes due. The IRS has a specific formula that can be applied to determine exactly how much the bonus needs to be "grossed up" to give the employee a full tax-free benefit.

Assuming the employee holds onto the shares (instead of selling them immediately), he or she will recognize a capital gain (if the stock price has risen) or loss (if the stock price has fallen) at the time the shares are sold, in an amount equal to the difference between the fair market value at grant and the sale price.[4] If the employee holds the shares for more than a year before selling them, he or she will be taxed, to the extent tax is due, at the lower long-term capital gains rates.

---

4.   Code Section 1202 provides for a 50% exclusion (60% for businesses in "empowerment zones") for gains from the sale of qualifying "small business stock" acquired in exchange for money, property, or services performed and held for at least five years. However, the balance (50%) is taxed at a capital gains rate of 28%, giving an effective tax rate of 14%, whereas the capital gains rate for those in middle and upper tax brackets is currently 15%. Given this slight 1 percentage point advantage, the various businesses that are excluded from qualifying under Section 1202, and the fact that part of the excluded gain is a tax preference item under the alternative minimum tax (AMT), this provision is not very significant.

It is important, even with financially sophisticated employees, to communicate the tax consequences of a direct stock grant. It is easy for someone to receive a piece of paper (i.e., the stock grant) and not realize that he or she now owes thousands of dollars in taxes as a result—and that the company will withhold those taxes. Furthermore, ending up with an unexpected obligation to pay those taxes can be de-motivating, achieving the opposite effect than was hoped for with the grant.

If the company is an S corporation, the employee receiving the shares will, as long as he or she retains them, be responsible for paying his or her proportionate share of taxes on corporate earnings. As is often the case with S corporations, however, the company may pay distributions to cover the tax cost.

Employer Considerations

The company is eligible for a compensation deduction in the amount the employee recognizes as ordinary income (i.e., the fair market value of the shares when granted), to the extent the amount constitutes reasonable compensation.

The company must report this amount as wages on the employee's Form W-2 and withhold taxes on the grant; if a cash bonus is added to the grant to pay for taxes, the cash bonus may be used for withholding. In fact, the company may simply make the cash part of the total stock-plus-cash bonus equal to the withholding obligation. The company must pay employment taxes, just as with the employee's regular salary.

For financial accounting purposes, the company will recognize a compensation expense for the fair market value of the stock at grant (plus any cash bonus added to the grant). The increase in the number of company shares outstanding means that earnings per share will correspondingly decrease, all other things being equal.

Deferred Compensation (Section 409A) Issues

Direct stock grants are generally not subject to the deferred compensation rules under Code Section 409A, which a later chapter discusses in detail.

Advantages of Direct Stock Grants

• Unlike tax-qualified plans such as ESOPs (discussed in a later chapter) or Section 423 ESPPs (discussed below), a direct stock grant program gives the employer a great deal of flexibility in deciding who gets what.

• The company may provide that the stock must be sold back to it, so it can ensure that ownership does not become too widely distributed.

• The employee receives immediate, direct, and real ownership, unlike the case with many other stock plans, and being an actual shareholder may suit the company's goals. For example, with stock options, the employee receives a chance to purchase shares in the future, and often chooses to sell those shares immediately for a quick profit, so the period when the employee is a shareholder is very brief. Similarly, with Section 423 ESPPs, employees often immediately sell the shares to gain a profit on the difference between a discounted purchase price and the current market value of the stock. With phantom stock and SARs settled in cash, no equity is transferred. With ESOPs, the employee has no direct ownership until and unless shares are distributed to him or her, which is usually after termination and usually is followed by a resale back to the company. It is possible to have a direct stock grant that is immediately resold by the employee, but as noted above, the company can simply place restrictions on the resale of the shares.

• Many employees may not want to buy company stock, especially if they lack the funds or are cautious due to financial advice not to put all of one's eggs in the same basket (i.e., to both invest in a company and depend on it for one's salary), especially in a post-Enron world. A direct stock grant avoids this problem by simply giving the stock to employees.

• Because a direct stock grant is conceptually simple, it presents no problems for employee comprehension. (As noted above, however, the company must ensure that employees realize the grant is taxable upon receipt.)

Disadvantages of Direct Stock Grants

- The employee recognizes income for tax purposes immediately upon the receipt of the grant. This may be a disheartening experience for employees, especially if they must hold the shares for some time, they have difficulty in paying the taxes that are due (and the company does not help finance the tax burden), or the company has not adequately communicated the tax consequences.

- If the company is an S corporation and the company does not make distributions to cover shareholder taxes, the employee will have to pay his or her proportionate share of corporate taxes.

- Real ownership means the employee is a shareholder, with the voting rights (to the extent the class of stock used has voting rights) and privileges that entails. In some cases, the company may find this undesirable, but as noted above, it should not be a serious issue.

- Because the shares are free and not subject to vesting or performance restrictions, one objection is that the employee has no "skin in the game" and will be less likely to be motivated than in the case of stock programs that require the employee to pay for shares and/or be subject to forfeiture conditions.

- If the company is an S corporation, then, as with all incentive programs that result in the transfer of actual shares, the company must ensure that the limit on the number of shareholders (100 as of this writing[5]) is not exceeded, or the S election will terminate immediately.[6]

- Issuing new shares to grant to employees will dilute the company stock, which, as with other equity programs that cause dilution, may displease existing shareholders.

- Since the grant of shares is treated like compensation, the employer must pay employment taxes on the grant. Employers must pay all federal unemployment taxes (FUTA) and state

---

5. See Code Section 1361(b)(1)(A).

6. Treasury Regulations Section 1.1362-2(b).

employment taxes, and they must pay a matching amount for Social Security and Medicare taxes (FICA).

- If the company is private, it will have to decide how the employee can dispose of the shares sooner or later and thus profit from them; otherwise, they will have little incentive value (although the company could pay dividends on them). If the company restricts employees' sale of the stock, the employees may value the award less, but if the company agrees to freely buy back the stock, it could face cash-flow issues if many employees want to sell at once.

Direct Stock Purchases

As noted above, simply giving stock to the employee is not necessarily the best choice (although sometimes it may be). A company may wish to sell shares to employees instead. This part of the chapter discusses simple, direct stock sales; the next section of the chapter addresses formal ESPPs.

Direct stock sales are mainly used in private companies; in public companies, employees can simply purchase shares on the open market, or, if a discount is desired, the company can provide for an ESPP with a discount.

Many of the same considerations stated above with respect to no-cost stock grants apply here; for example, a private company will have to decide how employees can dispose of shares they acquire; an S corporation will have to ensure that the limit on the maximum number of shareholders is not exceeded; and so on.

Tax and Accounting Treatment of Direct Stock Purchases

Employee Considerations

When the employee purchases stock, he or she recognizes ordinary income for tax purposes to the extent that a discount was given. Thus, if no discount is given, there is no taxable income at that time; if there is, say, a $5 per share discount, then the employee recognizes $5 per share of ordinary income. (As discussed in the chapter on restricted stock, when an employee buys stock subject to vesting, the employee recognizes income only when the stock vests unless the Section 83(b) election is made.) Any cash bonus given to help pay taxes will be taxed itself.

As with other stock that an employee holds, he or she will recognize a capital gain (if the stock price has risen) or loss (if the stock price falls) at the time the shares are sold, in an amount equal to the difference between the fair market value at grant and the sale price. If the employee holds the shares for over a year before selling them, he or she will be taxed, to the extent tax is due, at the lower long-term capital gains rates.

As with direct stock grants, it is important, even with financially sophisticated employees, to communicate the tax consequences of a direct stock purchase. For example, the employee may purchase stock at its fair market value and recognize no income, but if the company is an S corporation, the employee will, as long as he or she retains the shares, be responsible for paying his or her proportionate share of taxes on corporate earnings.

Employer Considerations

The company is eligible for a compensation deduction to the extent the employee recognizes ordinary income due to a discount on the stock price. The company must report any such amount as wages on the employee's Form W-2 and withhold taxes on the grant; if a cash bonus is added to the grant to pay for taxes, the cash bonus (which becomes part of the ordinary income reported as wages and subject to withholding) may be used for withholding. The company must pay employment taxes, just as with the employee's regular salary.

For financial accounting purposes, the company will recognize a compensation expense only to the extent the stock is sold at a discount and/or to the extent that the purchase is coupled with a cash bonus to help pay any taxes.

Deferred Compensation (Section 409A) Issues

Direct stock purchases in which the release of shares to the purchaser is not deferred are not subject to the deferred compensation rules under Code Section 409A.

Advantages

A direct stock purchase plan shares several advantages with a direct stock grant:

- The company can be flexible in determining who gets what.
- The company can provide that stock must be sold back to it.
- The employee receives immediate and real ownership.
- A direct stock purchase is conceptually simple for employees to understand.

However, there are differences arising from the fact that the employee pays for the shares:

- With a direct stock purchase, the employee must put some "skin in the game" by buying the stock. For companies concerned that a free stock grant would be a meaningless giveaway, this is a major consideration.
- Related to this is the fact that paying for the stock means the employee will not be shocked by receiving "free" stock that carries a hidden price tag in the form of income tax paid on the value of the shares. If there is no discount, then no income will be recognized when the shares are bought.
- Similarly, when the employee pays the full fair market of the shares, the employer is not responsible for employment taxes (FUTA, etc.), unlike with direct stock grants.
- The sale of stock generates money for the company.

Disadvantages

As with the advantages discussed above, direct stock purchase plans share several disadvantages with direct stock grants:

- In S corporations, the employee will be responsible for his or her share of corporate taxes as long as the employee holds the stock, and the company must ensure that the statutory limit on the number of S corporation shareholders is not exceeded.

- The employee will have voting rights to the extent the stock has such rights.

- Issuing new shares to sell to employees will dilute the company stock, which may displease existing shareholders.

- If the company is private, it will have to decide how the employee can dispose of the shares.

As with the advantages, the fact that the employee pays for the shares creates what may be viewed as a disadvantage:

- Employees, especially lower-paid employees, may be reluctant to participate in a program that makes them pay for the shares. This is one reason why a direct stock purchase program is often associated with executives or other key employees, not with broader groups of employees.

Employee Stock Purchase Plans (ESPPs)

An ESPP creates a formal structure for employees to buy stock from their employer, usually at specified points and at a discount, via payroll deductions. Most ESPPs are tax-qualified plans governed by Section 423 of the Internal Revenue Code, but some ESPPs are nonqualified plans.

Mainly for Public Companies

If you are in a private company, you should know at the outset that ESPPs are mainly used in public companies. A typical ESPP provides for ongoing automatic purchases of shares whose fair market value is automatically calculated. For a public company, the stock market provides the share value at any given time, employees can easily sell their shares (which they sometimes will arrange to do automatically to take a quick profit), and the whole process can be easily facilitated by a designated broker and transfer agent. In a private company, however, the fair market value is not a given but rather something that must be established for a given date through an appraisal or other reliable process; the company must either register the securities or comply with an exemption from securities registration; there is no public market for shares the employees want to sell, and the company may not want to repurchase the shares; employees may not even want to enroll in the automatic purchase of shares they cannot sell on the market; and there are typically no institutions in place such as a transfer agent that can be called upon to facilitate the ESPP stock purchasing process.

How ESPPs Work

In a typical ESPP, employees enroll in the plan and designate how much will be deducted from their paychecks. During an "offering period," the participating employees have funds regularly deducted from their pay (on an after-tax basis) and held in designated accounts in preparation for the stock purchase. At the end of the offering period, each participant's accumulated funds are used to buy shares, usually at a specified discount (up to 15%) from the market value. It is very common to have a "look-back" feature in which the price the employee pays is based on the lower of the price at the beginning of the offering period or the price at the end of the offering period.

Usually, an ESPP allows participants to withdraw from the plan before the offering period ends and have their accumulated funds returned to them. It is also common to allow participants who remain in the plan to change the rate of their payroll deductions as time goes on.

Although ESPPs operate differently from incentive or nonqualified stock options, you may see them referred to as options. Code Section 423 terms the opportunity to participate in an ESPP an "option," the beginning of the offering period the "grant date," and the purchase the "exercise." Section 423 plans and incentive stock options (ISOs) are collectively referred to as "statutory stock options."

Section 423 ESPPs

As noted above, the vast majority of ESPPs are tax-qualified "Section 423" plans. Employees participating in Section 423 ESPPs are eligible for favorable tax treatment if certain requirements are met. Under Section 423, an ESPP must be designed and operate as follows:

- Only employees of the company or its parent or subsidiaries may participate.

- The company's stockholders must approve the plan within 12 months before or after its adoption.

- Employees who own 5% or more of the company's stock may not participate.

- All employees, except for 5%-or-more owners, must be able to participate, except for those employed less than two years, those whose customary employment is 20 hours or less per week, those who work for not more than five months per year, and "highly compensated" employees as defined in Code Section 414(q).

- All employees must have equal rights and privileges under the plan, except that the amount of stock they can purchase may bear a uniform relationship to compensation.

- The purchase price cannot be less than the lesser of 85% of the fair market value (1) at the beginning of the offering period or (2) at the purchase date.

- The maximum term of an offering period under the ESPP may not exceed 27 months unless the purchase price is based only on the fair market value at the time of purchase, in which case the offering periods may be up to five years long.

- No participant may receive a grant allowing his or her rights to purchase stock under all Section 423 plans of the employer (and its parent and subsidiary corporations) to accrue at a rate exceeding $25,000 worth of stock per year, determined using the fair market value at the beginning of the offering period.

- The right to buy stock must be nontransferable except by will or the laws of descent and distribution, and during the employee's life this right must be exercisable only by the employee.

Tax Treatment of Employees

With a Section 423 plan, as with ISOs, the employee is taxed only upon the disposition of the stock, and capital gains treatment is available if a holding period is satisfied. Unlike the case with qualifying dispositions of ISOs, however, there is an ordinary income element, and the Section 423 rules can lead to unusual results. As with ISOs, there is a special holding period of one year after the purchase date and two years after the beginning of the offering period that determines the employee's tax treatment. If the employee sells the shares after the end of the holding period, the sale is a "qualifying disposition." If the employee sells the shares before the holding period ends, the sale is a "disqualifying disposition," and the tax treatment is different.

If the employee satisfies the holding period and has a qualifying disposition, he or she owes ordinary income tax on the lesser of (1) the discount element applied to the fair market value of the stock at the beginning of the offering period (i.e., the "grant date") or (2) the sale price minus the purchase price. Any other gain or loss is a long-term capital gain or loss.

If the employee does not hold the shares for the holding period and thus has a disqualifying disposition, the employee owes ordinary income tax on the difference between the fair market value at purchase and the actual purchase price. Any other gain or loss is a short- or long-term capital gain or loss, depending on how long the stock is held before being sold (it is long-term if the stock is held for more than a year).

For example, suppose that Susan is an employee of a company offering a Section 423 plan. She enrolls in the plan and elects to have $100 deducted from each paycheck. The plan has a 15% discount, a look-back provision, and a 12-month offering period. The stock price is $20 when the offering period begins. Susan does not withdraw from the ESPP, so at the end of the offering period, a stock purchase is automatically made on her behalf using the accumulated funds. The stock price at that time is $25. Because the plan has a look-back provision, the discount is taken from the lower of the price at the beginning of the offering period or at the end, so her price per share is $17 (85% of $20, the price at the beginning). She later sells the shares for $30, for a profit of $13.

If Susan holds the shares for the holding period before selling them, she will have a qualifying disposition. She will recognize ordinary income of $3 per share (the lesser of the 15% discount applied to the share value at the beginning of the offering period [$20 share value x .15 = $3], and the sale price minus the purchase price [$30 sale price - $17 purchase price = $13]). The remainder of her profit ($10 per share) is taxed at the long-term capital gains rate.

If, on the other hand, Susan does not hold the shares for the holding period before selling them, she will have a disqualifying disposition. She will recognize $8 per share in ordinary income ($25 share value at purchase - $17 purchase price). The remaining $5 per share is taxed as a capital gain, which will be short- or long-term depending on how long she held the shares.

The Section 423 rules can lead to interesting outcomes. For example, if the employee sells at a loss because the stock price has fallen below the purchase price, you might think that no tax should be due, and in fact this is the case with a qualifying disposition. However, if the employee sells before the end of the holding period and thus has a disqualifying disposition, he or she will still have to pay tax on the difference between the share value at purchase and the purchase price. Here, the employee must weigh the risk of paying taxes due to a disqualifying disposition against the risk of ending up with near-worthless shares if he or she continues to hold them so as to have a qualifying disposition.

In another interesting outcome, if the stock price falls during the offering period but then rises before the employee sells the shares, a disqualifying disposition sometimes results in *better* tax treatment if it has a smaller ordinary income element and a larger capital gain element than a qualifying disposition. Example: In an ESPP with a 15% discount, the stock price falls from $20 to $10 during the offering period and then rises to $15 when the employee sells the shares, which were bought for $8.50 each (a 15% discount from $10). The ordinary income element is $3 per share for a qualifying disposition (the lesser of the 15% discount at the beginning of the offering period and the actual profit of $6.50) and $1.50 per share for a disqualifying disposition (the share price at the end of the offering period minus the purchase price). The employee with a disqualifying disposition in this situation can take advantage of the larger capital gains element either by holding the shares for at least a year before sale so as to receive long-term capital gains treatment or by having capital losses that he or she can apply to offset even a short-term capital gain.

Tax Treatment of Employer

With a qualifying disposition, the employer receives no tax deduction. With a disqualifying disposition, the employer receives a tax deduction to the extent that the employee recognizes ordinary income. Ordinary income from a disqualifying disposition is reported on the employee's W-2 form and to the IRS (the company must do this to receive its tax deduction). No income tax withholding or payroll (FICA/FUTA) tax withholding is required.[7]

Deferred Compensation (Section 409A) Issues

The Section 409A deferred compensation rules do not apply to Section 423 plans, but they can apply to nonqualified ESPPs, as discussed below.

Design and Accounting Considerations

Although Section 423 sets forth many limits on plan design, employers still have flexibility in designing plans. For example, they can choose:

- How many shares to make available for the plan (there is no statutory limit).

- Whether everyone can purchase the same amount of shares or whether there will be a per-person limit based on each person's level of compensation.

- Whether there is a look-back provision.

---

7. This used to be contested by the IRS, but the American Jobs Creation Act of 2004 settled the issue.

- The size of the discount (from zero to 15%) and, if there is a look-back provision, whether the discount is the same at both the beginning of the offering period and on the purchase date.

- The length and structure of the offering period (for example, there can be multiple overlapping offering periods, each of which has several interim purchase dates within it).

- Whether an offering period of over a year with interim purchase dates will allow a participant to avoid buying stock during the first year but accrue up to the yearly maximum ($25,000 worth of stock measured as of the beginning of the offering period) to use in a subsequent year of the same offering period (for example, $50,000 worth of stock in the second year of a 24-month offering period).

Financial accounting rules affect design considerations. The accounting standard for equity compensation in the U.S., Statement of Financial Accounting Standards No. 123 (revised 2004) (FAS 123(R)), which went into effect in 2005 and 2006, draws a distinction between "compensatory" and "noncompensatory" plans. Compensatory plans result in a compensation expense on a company's balance sheet (based on a calculation of the purchase right's "fair value"—for example, a higher discount will result in a higher fair value), while noncompensatory plans do not. This matters most to public companies, which are exactly the kind of companies that sponsor ESPPs. An ESPP is noncompensatory under FAS 123(R) if it meets the following criteria:[8]

- There are no "option-like" features such as a look-back provision.

- If a discount on company stock is offered to ESPP participants but not shareholders, the ESPP discount must not exceed the reasonable cost of raising capital; a 5% safe harbor is allowed.

---

8. The previous accounting standard, APB Opinion No. 25, was more generous in categorizing ESPPs as noncompensatory. Under Opinion No. 25, all Section 423 plans (and thus most ESPPs) were considered noncompensatory and thus resulted in no accounting expense.

- Substantially all employees who meet limited employment quali-fications are eligible to participate on an equitable basis.

The new accounting rules have forced ESPP sponsors to choose between offering attractive features traditionally associated with most ESPPs (look-back provisions and deeper-than-5% discounts) on one hand and minimizing the compensation expense shown on their balance sheets on the other hand.[9] In a 2006 NCEO survey of ESPP sponsors, 12% had discontinued or decided to discontinue their ESPP due to FAS 123(R)'s expensing requirements. Twenty-eight percent were eliminating a look-back feature, and 22% were lowering the discount percentage (usually to 5% or less) or even eliminating it.[10]

International Considerations

A Section 423 plan sponsor with non-U.S. employees can run into problems when Section 423's strict participation requirements mandate the inclusion of non-U.S. employees whose countries require special treatment that in turn violates the Section 423 requirement to provide everyone with equal rights and privileges under the plan. This is a complex area, but generally speaking, the company can avoid these problems if the non-U.S. employees are in foreign subsidiaries that are omitted from the plan. A similar but nonquali-fied version of the U.S.-based plan may be created to benefit the employees thus excluded from participation.

---

9. Another example of FAS 123(R)'s effect on plan design is to discourage the use of a formerly popular feature in which a fall in the stock price triggered a "reset" or "automatic low offering period" provision terminating the offer-ing period at the next purchase date and enrolling the participants in a new offering period at the now-low stock price. Under FAS 123(R), this is treated as a modification and thus as a cancellation of the old ESPP option and the grant of a new one, resulting in additional accounting expense.

10. National Center for Employee Ownership, *2006 ESPP Survey*, published on-line.

Nonqualified Plans

Some ESPPs are not qualified under Section 423. For example, a company may wish to design its plan to limit coverage to a certain class of employees or to treat classes of employees unequally in a way prohibited by Section 423. Alternatively, a plan may be drafted as a Section 423 plan but be operated in a way that violates the statutory restrictions and thus disqualifies the plan. There are no rules for designing or operating nonqualified plans and no special tax benefits.

Tax Treatment of Employee

Employees are taxed as they would be for nonqualified stock options: the employee recognizes ordinary income as of the date of purchase (not the date the stock is later sold, as with Section 423 plans) in the amount, if any, that the fair market value on that date exceeds the purchase price. Any subsequent appreciation or depreciation in value is treated as a capital gain or loss (which will be long-term if the stock is held at least a year) when the stock is later sold.

Section 409A and Employee Taxation

Most ESPPs offer discounts, as noted above. However, unlike Section 423 ESPPs, nonqualified ESPPs are not exempt from coverage under the Code Section 409A deferred compensation rules. Under these rules, discounted stock options (purchase rights under ESPPs are options for this purpose) constitute deferred compensation and are subject to Section 409A. The recipient of a stock option that is discounted below the share price at grant is subjected to ordinary income tax, penalty taxes, and interest at vesting unless the option complies with Section 409A's rules for deferral elections and the timing of distributions.[11] For example, a discounted option that by its terms must be exercised at vesting (or up to March 15 following the calendar year of vesting) will not incur Section 409A's penalties.

---

11. As noted elsewhere in this book, only nonqualified options can be granted at a discount to fair market value.

For a regular nonqualified stock option, this limit on the exercise date removes one of the most desirable features of stock options—being able to wait, perhaps years, for an opportune time to exercise. However, for an ESPP option, this is no problem; a typical ESPP is set up so that at specified dates, the "options" (purchase rights) are "vested" and are "exercised." Thus, a nonqualified ESPP that offers a discount to employees will be subject to Section 409A's rules, but it can be designed to avoid violating Section 409A and incurring the tax penalties thereunder.

Tax Treatment of Employer

The amount the employee recognizes as ordinary income is subject to withholding and to reporting on Form W-2. The employer receives a tax deduction for that amount as of the time of the purchase.

Advantages of ESPPs

- As with direct stock purchase programs, ESPP participation makes an employee put some "skin in the game" by investing in company stock.

- The sale of stock generates money for the company.

- For public companies, ESPPs are an ideal way to facilitate broad-based employee stock purchases.

- If a Section 423 plan is used, it offers tax-advantaged treatment for employees.

Disadvantages of ESPPs

- Unlike other equity compensation plans, Section 423 ESPPs must be offered to virtually all employees and on an equal basis. They cannot be used to reward individual or group performance.

- For closely held companies, the issues discussed near the beginning of this section mean that a typical ESPP operated as a payroll deduction plan is unlikely to be a good choice.

- Even in public companies, there is often a low participation rate in the ESPP,[12] presumably because many (or most) employees do not want to have money taken from their paychecks to buy stock.

- The main features that have made ESPPs advantageous to employees—look-back provisions and generous discounts—now cause the company to incur an accounting expense under FAS 123(R).

- If the ESPP is nonqualified, the Section 409A deferred compensation issues must be carefully addressed to avoid unpleasant tax consequences for employees.

Special Issues for Closely Held Companies

It is expensive for a company to go public and comply with the various rules for public companies, but having done that, the company will have little problem with several issues that can vex private companies. To establish the fair market value of the shares, a public company and its employees can simply look to the current price on the public stock market. Similarly, public company employees can go to the public stock market to sell their shares, at least if the stock is not so thinly traded that such sales are difficult. And for public company securities that have been registered, no exemption from registration is required. Closely held companies, and especially companies that are purely private (i.e., that are not publicly traded), on the other hand, face special issues, as discussed below.

Liquidity: How Will Employees Sell Their Shares?

If the company is not publicly traded or is so thinly traded that reselling shares is difficult, it must consider what the market for shares will be. Will employees sell shares to the company? Will employees be expected to hold the shares for an anticipated initial public offering (IPO) or an acquisition by another company? In any case,

---

12. National Center for Employee Ownership, *2006 ESPP Survey.*

the company must decide how the employees will end up getting income from the shares they receive.

If the company remains private, there are several alternatives. In a private company, each alternative raises the valuation issues mentioned below.

- The company can buy back the shares.

- The company could create a formal or informal internal market for shares. This can become quite expensive and is discussed elsewhere in this book.

- An ESOP can serve as the market (or one of the markets) for shares that employees have received from other plans. People often think of an ESOP as a means for a sole or main shareholder to sell a large block of stock, but there are no actual restrictions on the number of shareholders the ESOP can buy from. Thus, if the company has an ESOP, the ESOP can buy shares that were granted or sold to employees. And whereas the company would generally not receive a tax deduction for redeeming stock from employees, its contributions to an ESOP (to enable the ESOP to buy the shares from employees) are tax-deductible.

If the company is to repurchase the shares from employees, it must consider potential cash flow issues that might arise. Say, for example, that a stock grant agreement provides that employees can sell their shares to the company within 30 days of termination of employment and receive immediate payment at the then-current fair market value of the shares. (Indeed, the company might *require* employees to sell their shares back to the company after termination, as noted above.) Suppose that employees with grants representing a large number of shares leave precisely when the company has cash-flow problems; in such a situation, the company may be hard-pressed to satisfy its obligations. (Closely held companies that sponsor ESOPs are familiar with planning for the repurchase obligation that the ESOP creates, as discussed in the chapter of this book that covers ESOPs.) Similarly, cash-flow problems could arise if employees can sell back their shares at any time, even while still employed, and a surge in the value of the company (and thus the price they will receive) prompts a large number of them to sell their shares back. Even if the ESOP or internal market solutions mentioned above are used, a sudden flood of stock for sale could create a strain on the company.

Valuation Issues

As noted above, valuation is not an issue in a public company. But in a private company, a stock transfer to or from employees raises the issue of how the stock is to be valued—for example, in calculating the tax due, the deduction to be taken, the price to be paid when repurchasing the shares, and so on. Aside from obtaining a formal appraisal, private companies have used a wide range of simpler and cheaper valuation methods, such as assigning a nominal value per share; using a formula or formulas based on earnings, etc.; pricing common stock at a given fraction of the price of preferred stock sold in recent rounds of funding; or using a price negotiated with a third-party buyer as a benchmark.

The stock grants and stock purchase programs discussed in this chapter do not have any specific valuation requirements. In contrast, with an ESOP (mentioned above as a possible mechanism for repurchasing shares from employees), a formal appraisal from an independent, qualified appraiser is required by law to ensure that the ESOP does not pay more than fair market value for the shares. And for nonqualified stock options and stock appreciation rights (SARs), regulations under Section 409A of the Internal Revenue Code impose specific valuation requirements for exemption from Section 409A's application.

Just because stock grants and stock purchase programs do not have legal valuation requirements, however, does not mean that you can pick a number out of a hat without facing unpleasant consequences. For example, a private company that plans to go public may face "cheap stock" securities issues. If the Securities and Exchange Commission (SEC) believes that equity grants, especially those given in the 12 months or so before the initial public offering, were priced below fair market value (i.e., were "cheap"), the

SEC will force the company to record a compensation expense that reflects the underpricing.

Even if the company has no plans to go public, a faulty valuation can cause severe problems, even if it is too high instead of too low. If the shares are priced too high, then even with a free grant of shares, the employee is paying too much in tax, and the company is paying too much in employment taxes. And if the employees buy the shares, they will pay too much—and will likely be angry if a formal valuation made later on shows that to be the case. Or take the case of a grant designed to give the employee shares equal to a given percentage of pay; if the shares are priced too cheaply, the company will be giving away too much equity to employees. Another example is structuring a stock grant or stock sale program so that shares are awarded at book value and later resold to the company at book value. Since book value (basically, assets minus liabilities) is often not equal to the real fair market value of a company, employees in this case will miss out on the true increase in value of the shares, subverting the purpose and promise behind equity sharing.

Valuation is a complex subject. Although many private companies have eschewed formal appraisals and used the simple approaches such as those named above, those simple approaches by their very nature can oversimplify the issues at hand. Consider, for example, that any two shares of the same company, even if they are both common shares (as opposed to preferred shares) may have a much different fair market value. One share may have different voting rights, different resale restrictions, different dividend privileges, and so on. And even if those rights and privileges are all the same, a block of stock representing a controlling interest is worth more per share than a minority interest in the company.

Given the complexity and implications of the issues involved, we at the NCEO recommend that private companies give serious thought to hiring a professional appraiser to value the stock for their equity compensation programs, even if they do not plan to go public for the foreseeable future. (Of course, a company that already has an ESOP presumably already employs an appraiser, and that appraiser could be called upon to arrive at a fair market value for the non-ESOP equity grants.) For more information on valuation and the methods used to value companies, see the section on valuation in the deferred compensation chapter of this book.

Securities Laws

As noted above, improper "cheap" valuations of equity grants can raise issues with the SEC when going public. The main securities-related issues, however, are those pertaining to the sale of shares that have not been registered under a public offering. Because direct stock grants (at no cost to employees) do not constitute "sales" of securities, they are exempt from registration requirements. The discussion below thus pertains to direct stock sales and stock purchase plans. For more information, see the chapter on securities issues.

If a private company wishes to sell its securities, whether to employees or others, it must either meet federal and state registration requirements or fit into an applicable exemption. Registration can be very expensive (often costing well over $100,000) and makes the company subject to detailed reporting requirements, so a company that is not going public almost invariably will want to use an exemption from registration. Perhaps the most popular registration exemption for equity compensation programs under federal law is SEC Rule 701, under which offers of securities to employees, directors, and certain others are exempt if sales during a 12-month period do not exceed the greater of (1) $1 million, (2) 15% of the issuer's total assets, or (3) 15% of the total amount of the class of securities being offered. There also are other exemptions, such as Rules 504, 505, and 506 under Regulation D, but Rule 701 is generally more advantageous for employee stock plans. In addition to exemption under federal law, the company will have to meet exemptions under applicable state securities laws (commonly called "blue sky" laws), and the laws of more than one state may apply.

Shares that have not been offered pursuant to a registration statement, i.e., a public offering, are called "restricted securities"; do not confuse this with "restricted stock" grants, which are stock grants with restrictions such as vesting. Just as the *company* needs an exemption to sell restricted securities, an *employee* or other person who is given or sold restricted securities by the company needs to fit within an exemption if he or she is to resell the shares. The employee may freely resell the shares back to the company. To resell to others, the employee must follow SEC Rule 144 (the most commonly applicable exemption for sales by recipients of restricted securities) or another exemption, assuming the securities are not subsequently registered.

Aside from rules regarding the sale of securities, there are federal and state anti-fraud rules that apply to every securities transaction. Under the anti-fraud rules, oral and written statements about the company and its securities must not be false or misleading.

Conclusion

Direct stock sales, stock grants, and stock purchase plans can play an important part in a company's equity compensation strategy, but you must remember to weigh their pros and cons. Direct stock grants are a good example of something that seems an obvious solution to many but in fact comes with lots of strings attached (like tax liability for both the employee and the company). And if you are a closely held company, do not forget the special valuation, securities, and other issues that apply.

CHAPTER 3

Restricted Stock Awards and Restricted Stock Units

COREY ROSEN

Restricted stock awards (RSAs) and restricted stock units (RSUs) have become increasingly popular ways to compensate employees. Often used just for key employees, they can also be provided more broadly. RSAs and RSUs can also be provided to non-employees, such as contractors and board members.

Restricted stock plans provide employees with the right to purchase shares at fair market value or at a discount, or employees may receive shares at no cost. However, the shares employees acquire are not really theirs yet—they cannot take possession of them until specified restrictions lapse (or, put another way, their awards vest). Most commonly, the restrictions lapse if the employee continues to work for the company for a certain number of years, often three to five. The time-based restrictions may lapse all at once or gradually—for example 20% per year over five years. The company can impose any restrictions, however. It could, for instance, restrict the shares until certain corporate, departmental, or individual performance goals are achieved. There can also be "double triggers," meaning both a time-based requirement and a performance requirement must be met. In some private companies, the restriction is both time-based and transaction-based, meaning the restrictions don't lapse until the company goes public or is sold. While the shares are subject to restrictions, companies can choose whether to pay dividends, provide voting rights, or give the employee other benefits of being a shareholder. Any shares that do not vest are forfeited.

RSAs are generally issued at grant but the awards are held in an escrow account until they vest. With RSUs, the company does not actually issue the shares until the restrictions lapse. The same kinds of vesting rules apply, but as we will see, the tax treatment is slightly different. RSUs have the same effect as phantom stock settled in shares instead of cash and do not carry voting or dividend rights until the employee actually takes possession of the shares, although a kind of tracking dividend can be paid in the form of a bonus.

The growing popularity of RSAs and RSUs is largely a function of changes in accounting rules and greater shareholder concern about dilution. Until recent accounting changes, companies preferred to use stock options because they did not have to charge their cost as a compensation expense, while RSAs and RSUs did require such accounting. Now that all plans are treated as costs, companies are looking again at restricted stock.

In addition, restricted stock appears less dilutive because restricted stock grants are usually smaller than option grants for reasons described below. When a company issues options, shareholders count overhang, which is one way of measuring dilution, as:

The number of shares that would need to be available to satisfy all outstanding unexercised equity compensation awards, regardless of whether they have vested

Plus

The number of shares authorized but not yet issued for new awards

Divided by

The total shares outstanding

For purposes of calculating diluted earnings per share, outstanding equity compensation awards are included, regardless of whether the awards have vested. However, authorized but not yet issued awards are not included.

So each stock option—or potential option—counts the same as a newly issued share, even if many options will never be exercised.

Because of the uncertainty about whether they will ever have value, companies need to issue many more options than "full value awards" such as RSAs or RSUs to achieve the same economic effect. A very broad rule of thumb is that because a restricted share has value even if the stock price goes down, while an option's future value requires the share price to rise, each restricted share is worth about three options. (This ratio varies considerably with each company, however.) So fewer restricted shares can be issued, causing less apparent dilution. Of course, if the two awards are economically equivalent, the economic dilution is, by definition, the same. Only dilution in the more nominal sense of the number of shares (but not their value) is different.

Some companies, most notably Microsoft and Amazon, have switched to RSUs for their broad-based plans because they are no longer rapid-growth companies. Thus, options provided a very uncertain future benefit to employees, while RSUs guarantee at least some value to the awards. Of course, what to recipients is a benefit of RSAs and RSUs, is to some people the problem with them—they reward people even if the share price does not go up.

Acquiring and Selling Shares

In public companies, restricted stock is almost always provided at no charge, or occasionally at a discount. An employee would have little incentive to buy restricted stock in a public company at fair market value when the same shares could be purchased on the open market for the same price with no restrictions. Closely held companies, however, often require employees to pay something for the stock. In many private companies, the price for the shares is very low and not a significant issue; in others, the incentive is simply the ability to own shares that would not otherwise be available. Employees generally have only a limited time to decide whether they will purchase restricted stock, usually not more than 30 days.

Employees can typically make the purchase with cash, existing shares, or both. The employer may also loan the money to the employee, subject to the usual tax rules about employee loans. A loan with an interest rate less than the applicable federal rate would be subject to taxation based on rules for imputed interest. The loan should be secured by the shares or some other security. Public companies, however, cannot make loans to top executives.

During the vesting period, restricted shares are not transferable. Private companies usually have a right of first refusal to repurchase the stock from the recipient. If the shares end up partially vested, the company has the right to repurchase the unvested shares at the price the employee paid for them or the current fair market value, whichever is lower.

In contrast, employees do not purchase RSUs. The fact that the shares are not actually issued until the vesting period ends is an advantage of RSUs over RSAs for companies that are concerned about minimizing the number of shares actually issued or that want to grant equity compensation to international employees in countries where issuing shares triggers immediate taxation regardless of vesting restrictions. In a public company, for the employee to buy the shares once they vest would be equivalent to buying them on the market, which the employee could have done at any prior time. In a closely held company, the only reason an employee might be willing to buy the shares after waiting for the right to vest is because of a strong desire to own shares otherwise unavailable. Few companies, however, would want to make an employee wait for some period of time before providing a right to buy stock, as opposed to letting them buy it up front and then restricting its vesting, as would be the case with RSAs.

In public companies, employees can sell their shares on the market. The company may want to repurchase any unvested shares that are forfeited so that it can make them available to other employees. But in closely held companies, the issue is more complicated. Employees may not see a benefit to receiving unmarketable shares on which they may have paid taxes and/or paid to purchase the shares in the first place. Companies could simply agree to repurchase the shares at the time the awards vest, but if they do that, should they bother with shares in the first place? If the employee did not pay for the shares at grant, immediate cash out of the shares makes them precisely equivalent to phantom stock. If the employee does pay something, of course, then the restricted stock differs from phantom stock, which never requires an advance employee purchase.

There are a variety of alternatives to immediate cash out. The company could make vesting contingent on a liquidity event, such as a sale of the company, a public offering, or the establishment of an ESOP that can buy the shares. In these circumstances, closely held companies commonly provide that they will repurchase stock held by employees who terminate before such an event at the price the employee paid for them or the shares' current value, whichever is lower. The company could also agree to repurchase the shares, in whole or in part, at some time after the awards vest. Employees might also be able to sell their shares to other employees or, with the employer's permission, to outside investors (although investors rarely want to buy small minority interests in closely held companies). However, the employee can resell the shares to someone other than the employer only if the shares are registered or if an exemption from registration is available.

Taxation

Recipients of RSAs pay ordinary income on the difference between the grant and exercise price when the restrictions lapse, e.g., when the award vests. RSU recipients pay income taxes when the award pays out—which is usually, but not always, on the vesting date. For awards granted at no cost to the employee, the taxable amount is the full value of the shares on the vesting date. Subsequent changes in value after the restrictions lapse are capital gains or losses.

The amount on which the employee is required to pay ordinary income tax is subject to payroll taxes and withholding. The compensation can be aggregated with the employee's other compensation or separately assessed using the flat rates for supplemental wage payments, such as bonuses. The taxes can be paid with a promissory note that carries at least the minimum interest rate required by federal law so as not to create imputed interest, by tendering shares, by cash, or using proceeds from selling some of the shares. In some cases, where the amounts due are relatively small, they could be withheld out of the employee's normal compensation.

When employees are awarded RSAs (but not RSUs), they have the right to make what is called a "Section 83(b)" election. If they make the election, they are taxed at ordinary income tax rates on the "bargain element" of the award at the time of grant. If the shares were simply granted to the employee, then the bargain element is their full value. The company gets a tax deduction to the extent the employee pays ordinary income tax. If the employee paid full value for the shares, then an 83(b) election allows him or her to freeze the ordinary income element at zero. If the employee paid less than fair market value for the shares, then the tax is based on the difference between what is paid and the fair market value at the time of the grant. The difference between the award price and any consideration paid is subject to withholding just like other compensation income. There is no additional tax until the shares are sold, when the difference between the award price and the sale price is taxed at capital gains rates.

For instance, say Mary gets the right to 100 restricted shares worth $50 per share in 2007. She pays $10 per share for them. Her bargain element is $40 per share, so she pays taxes on $40 x 100, or $4,000. The $40 per share bargain element is a tax deduction to the company. The shares vest in 2011, and Mary sells them in 2013 when they are worth $80 per share. She pays taxes on the gain at the time of sale. Her capital gain is $30 per share, and she pays tax at long-term capital gains rates on that. The company does not get a deduction for the capital gains income.

An 83(b) election is the obvious choice if the employee pays full value for the shares, because there is no ordinary income tax and future gains are taxed at capital gains rates. It may be a good choice as well if the employee is reasonably sure the stock will significantly rise in value, and the employee expects to meet the vesting require-ments. But 83(b) elections have one big drawback. The tax paid (in Mary's case, $4,000) cannot be refunded if the vesting requirements are not met and the shares are forfeited. Similarly, if the stock value goes down after the election, no deduction for the loss is available unless the shares are actually sold at a lower price. The result of all this is that employees generally only make the 83(b) election when they pay full value for the shares or are awarded shares that have only a nominal value. (Companies are free to tell employees that 83(b) elections are a possibility. However, they should be careful not to recommend a particular approach lest they be construed to be giving tax advice.)

With RSUs, employees cannot make the 83(b) election because no property changes hands until the shares are issued. Therefore, when the award vests and the employee receives the shares, the employee recognizes ordinary income, even though the shares have not yet been sold. The employer gets a corresponding deduction. If an employee has elected to defer payment of an RSU until sometime after the vesting date, then the ordinary income taxes are not due until the employee receives the payment, but FICA and FUTA employment taxes are due on the vesting date. Note, however, that such deferrals are subject to the deferred compensation rules associated with Internal Revenue Code Section 409A, which are discussed below.

Deferred Compensation Issues

Although RSAs are not subject to the deferred compensation rules connected with Code Section 409A, RSUs are subject to them. However, RSUs that provide for the receipt of shares within Code Section 409A's "short-term deferral" period (2.5 months after the end of the year of vesting) are generally considered to comply with Section 409A. Companies that do not want awards to pay out that quickly after vesting can allow employees to specify payout dates within 30 days of the grant date as long as the vesting date is at least a year away. If the employees dies, become permanently disabled, or there is a corporate change in control, the payout could occur sooner. Because the 409A rules provide for high levels of taxation and penalties on noncompliant awards, plans should be designed to comply with the tax rules.

Accounting

Companies account for RSAs and RSUs whose only restriction is vesting by determining the total compensation cost at the time the award is made and recognizing that amount over the vesting period. If vesting is contingent on performance, then the company estimates when the performance goal is likely to be achieved and recognizes the expense over the expected vesting period. As with stock options, the expense is determined on the grant date; unlike options, no option pricing model is needed to determine the amount that must be reflected on the income statement. If the employee is simply given 1,000 restricted shares worth $10 per share, then a $10,000 cost is incurred. If the employee buys the shares at fair market value, no charge is recorded; if there is a discount, that counts as a cost. Because the accounting is based on the initial cost, companies with low share prices will find that a vesting requirement for the award means their accounting charge will be very low even if the stock price goes up.

Valuation

In public companies, the value of shares granted under an award is determined by the market, but closely held companies must determine a value themselves. Unlike options or stock appreciation rights (SARs), there are no tax rules requiring specific approaches to valuation. Many companies simply use book value or a formula devised by the board, such as a multiple of earnings.

These simple approaches, however, almost never reflect the true value of a company. Book value represents a company's net assets, not its potential based on earnings and growth. Few companies have a book value greater than their value in terms of these factors. Formula-based approaches and rules of thumb assume that each company is pretty much alike. Two companies of the same size in the same industry may have stock prices that are very different multiples of earnings. Given that the award of RSAs or RSUs involves potentially very large amounts of money, it makes sense to pay for professional, independent assistance in determining an accurate value.

Securities Law Issues

The offer to sell stock triggers securities law rules, even if no one buys shares. If the company issues restricted stock at no cost, there are no immediate securities law implications because there is no offer to sell. If there is a cost, public companies can register their shares for the offer on a Form S-8, a simplified registration statement available for employee benefit plans. In private companies, the offer can be excluded from registration requirements under one of a number of exemptions, particularly Rule 701 under the Securities Act of 1933, which offers exemptions for offers to employees. Companies offering less than 15% of their equity in any 12-month period generally are covered by this rule. Special issues may apply if the company goes public. Details on securities laws can be found in the chapter on this issue in this book.

Restricted Stock Plan Advantages and Disadvantages

RSAs and RSUs have many advantages and disadvantages, as outlined below:

Advantages

- Awards can provide service or performance targets for employees to achieve before actually receiving shares or having the right to acquire shares.

- Awards can be granted and vest according to any rules the company prefers.

- Shares can carry dividend and/or voting rights, if the company chooses.

- Unlike stock options or SARs, restricted stock retains some value for employees even if the share price goes down after the grant date.

- Capital gains treatment is available on all or part of the gain on RSA shares, provided an 83(b) election is made. (This treatment is not available to holders of RSUs.)

- Restricted stock requires fewer shares to provide a similar level of benefit to options, because the awards have value even if the share price declines.

- Employers who prefer that employees pay at least something for their shares can design their RSAs (but generally not their RSUs) accordingly.

Disadvantages

- The restrictions may make ownership seem like an unlikely benefit. If an employee purchases shares, especially at the market price, but then cannot actually take possession of them until certain events occur, buying the shares may not seem very attractive.

- Restricted stock has no value unless there is or will be a market for the shares at some point. Employees must believe this is a real possibility, not just a corporate intention.

- The company cannot take a tax deduction for the value of the gain employees eventually realize if employees have made an 83(b) election to have the gain taxed as a capital gain.

- If the employee pays full value for the shares, the employee must use after-tax dollars to do so. If less than full value is paid, there is an immediate tax consequence if 83(b) treatment is chosen; if it is not, however, the employee must pay ordinary income tax at vesting even if the shares cannot be sold at the time.

- The 83(b) election can provide for ultimately lower taxation, but it carries risks for the employee if the stock price declines or the awards never vest.

Like all the other equity methods described in this book, RSAs or RSUs are neither inherently better nor worse than other awards. They do provide a method of equity compensation that was largely ignored in the days when options carried no accounting charge, but that now is deservedly getting a serious second look.

CHAPTER 4

Phantom Stock and Stock Appreciation Rights

COREY ROSEN

One of the most common calls we get at the National Center for Employee Ownership is from business owners who want employees to participate in the equity growth of the company but who are concerned about actually giving out shares. In some cases, the fear is that employees may end up with too much influence in the company. In others, the owners worry that there is no market for the shares. Sometimes the company wants to share equity rights with employees in other countries but doesn't want to navigate the often complex laws that govern equity plans in other legal systems. Businesses that do not have stock, such as partnerships or LLCs, may want an approach that allows for equity sharing without the potential pitfalls of sharing actual partnerships or memberships in the LLC. And in many cases, the desire is just for something really simple.

Phantom stock and stock appreciation rights (SARs) can address these issues. At the outset, however, we should note that giving employees options, restricted stock, or other direct equity awards is rarely a control risk. Employees almost never accumulate enough stock to have meaningful control power or even to trigger the minority shareholder rights that various state laws and corporate bylaws may provide, although this certainly could happen if enough equity were shared. The liquidity issue is also misleading. If closely held companies give employees awards paid out in actual shares, they can always make them liquid by buying them back, which is the precise economic equivalent of giving out the equity value of a share award or the increase in value in a stock option award.

That still leaves some compelling reasons to consider SARs and phantom stock, however. It is possible to settle (i.e., pay out) these awards in cash or shares. Stock-settled SARs have the same economic effect for recipients as a cashless exercise of stock options but are less dilutive because the company does not have to issue as many shares as it would with a similarly sized option grant. Stock-settled phantom stock is functionally the same as restricted stock units (RSUs), which are discussed in the chapter on restricted stock. This chapter looks at the issues surrounding these plans.

Phantom Stock and SARs Defined

SARs and phantom stock are very similar concepts. Both are bonus plans that grant not stock but rather the right to receive an award based on the value of the company's stock, hence the terms "appreciation rights" and "phantom." The awards can pay out in cash or stock.

A SAR is like a stock option without the stock: it generally can be exercised freely at a point after vesting (or upon the occurrence of a specified event) and before the end of its term. At exercise, the company pays the SAR plan participant the amount that the share price has appreciated between the grant date and the exercise date, multiplied by the number of shares specified in the grant.

In contrast, phantom stock is like a restricted stock award without the stock: the plan participant receives a "phantom" grant of hypothetical shares that provides him or her with the full value of the shares at a given date or upon the occurrence of a specified event. Phantom stock plans often credit the accounts of participants with dividends, in which case the ultimate payout reflects what a holder of actual shares would have received if such events occurred. If there are stock splits, phantom stock or SARs would normally be adjusted to reflect that change.

Unlike tax-qualified plans such as incentive stock options (ISOs), employee stock ownership plans (ESOPs), and Section 423 employee stock purchase plans (ESPPs), the form of SAR and phantom stock plans is not defined by law. As described below, they are flexible and can have a variety of features. However, the Section 409A deferred compensation rules impose certain restrictions that affect design decisions.

Plan Design

Eligibility

Companies can provide phantom stock or SARs to anyone—employees, board members, contractors, or anyone else. If a company makes these awards broadly available to employees, however, there is a chance they could be considered "qualified employee benefit plans" falling under the same legal umbrella as retirement plans governed by ERISA (the Employee Retirement Income Security Act of 1974, as amended), especially if they are designed to pay out only at or after termination of employment. If so, they would have to meet a variety of ERISA-based rules for testing plan operations to make sure they do not discriminate in favor of more highly compensated employees. These are the rules that govern ESOPs, 401(k) plans, profit sharing plans, and other retirement plans. Because they introduce a variety of constraints on plans designs, SARs and phantom stock plans should be designed so as not to fall under ERISA's rubric. That is not difficult to do. If the plans are designed so that the awards are paid out periodically, such as every three to five years when a particular tranche of awards vests, they would not be considered retirement plans. Many phantom stock and SARs plans are designed to pay out in this way, as opposed to at termination, retirement, or sale of the company, and so should not run afoul of these rules.

Plans that do restrict payout until termination, retirement, or sale of the company will avoid ERISA coverage if they fall into the exemption for a "top-hat plan," which is an unfunded[1] deferred compensation plan maintained primarily for "a select group of manage-

---

1.   In this context, "unfunded" means only that the employer has not irrevocably set aside assets to fund the plan, putting such assets beyond the reach of general creditors.

ment or highly compensated employees." Many practitioners believe that a good rule of thumb is that if 15% or fewer of all employees are eligible, the plan will qualify for the top-hat exemption.

Vesting

Vesting can be based on whatever criteria the employer chooses. Most plans use time-based vesting, typically not more than five years. Vesting may be "cliff" (all at once) or graduated. Many plans, however, are performance-vested, meaning they vest only when a certain individual, group, or corporate target is met. Phantom plans that condition the receipt of the award on meeting certain financial or other performance objective are sometimes also called "performance unit plans." A few plans provide vesting only on termination or sale of the company. Companies can also use "double triggers," meaning vesting occurs only when two requirements have been met, most typically both service and performance requirements.

Settlement Dates

Once the awards are fully vested, phantom stock usually has a specific settlement date when the award is paid out, whereas employees can typically choose when to exercise their vested SARs. Phantom stock and SARs, like nonstatutory stock options, result in income taxes when the employee receives the payout. Plan designers have flexibility to set payout dates or events but should be mindful of the deferred compensation tax rules associated with Code Section 409A. For SARs that are not designed to be exempt from deferred compensation rules and for phantom stock, that means an employer that wants to allow deferral beyond vesting should adhere to the rules on the timing of deferral elections discussed in the deferred compensation chapter of this book.

Settlement Form

SARs and phantom stock can be settled in cash or in shares. SARs that pay out in stock have more favorable accounting treatment than SARs that pay out in cash, as discussed briefly in the section on accounting in this chapter as well as in the separate chapter on accounting. Phantom stock awards settled in shares are essentially the same concept as RSUs. The common parlance is to refer to phantom stock when discussing awards paid out in cash, but RSUs when discussing those that pay out in shares. These are terms of art, however, not terms of law. In fact, some companies refer to phantom stock as "shadow" stock or some other term, often because they see "phantom" stock as almost pejorative.

Dividends, Voting Rights, and Other Shareholder Rights

Phantom stock may pay a kind of phantom dividend, a payment equal to the dividends an owner of that actual number of shares would receive. Because this is not an actual dividend, it would be taxed as ordinary income. SARs could in theory pay dividend equivalents as well, although this is a less common design feature (the dividends would be based on the underlying number of shares, and thus not specifically linked to the increase in share value). The payment must be separate from the payout of the award itself to avoid deferred compensation tax treatment.[2] When the payout is made, it is taxed as ordinary income to the employee and is deductible by the employer. Neither phantom stock nor SARs carry voting rights or other shareholder control rights.

Term

A SAR that can be exercised past its vesting date will have an expiration date beyond which it is no longer exercisable; that additional period constitutes its term. For instance, an award might provide for vesting after five years but allow exercise for up to 10 years.

Taxation

As noted above, phantom stock and SARs are taxable as income once the employee has received the payout. That means that once

---

2. The IRS considers direct dividends on unvested SARs and stock options to be tantamount to offering a discount on the exercise price. Under Code Section 409A, the recipients of discounted stock options and SARs are subject to steep taxes and penalties.

an award is exercised, it is taxable to the employee. The employee pays tax on the benefit received as if it were ordinary income; the employer gets a corresponding deduction.

Phantom stock is subject to the deferred compensation rules associated with Section 409A. SAR designers have a choice between granting SARs that are exempt from or comply with Section 409A. To be exempt, a SAR award must meet four requirements:

- The payout cannot be more than the difference between the stock's fair market value on the grant date and fair market value on the payout date, and must be made on the date of exercise.

- The grant price must be at or above the grant date fair market value.

- The number of shares covered by the award must be known on the grant date.

- The income cannot be deferred beyond the exercise date.

The employee can choose when to exercise this kind of SAR after vesting, making it much like a stock option except that the employee does not pay an exercise price.

Fair market value for this purpose is defined as the price of the shares on the public market when the award is issued, or, if there is no public market, as determined by an outside appraisal firm or through another approach the IRS deems "reasonable."

If the employer does not want to abide by these rules—for example, it wants the award's exercise price to be lower than the grant date fair market value or to determine the number of shares subject to the award some time after the grant date—then it can design a SAR award to comply with Section 409A. In that case, the employer will generally specify a payout date or event instead of allowing the employee to choose when to exercise the award. The timing of such payments is also subject to the rules regarding deferred payments, which are set out in the chapter on deferred compensation.

The holders of awards that are neither compliant with nor exempt from the deferred compensation rules face steep taxes and penalties.

Pricing

Because of the tax issues, the starting value of Section 409A-exempt SARs must be based on the fair market value of the shares on the grant date. Section 409A-compliant SARs can be issued at any price the company chooses, but given that their purpose is to track the appreciation of the value of shares, companies typically base their price on the market value of stock, an appraised value, a fair market equivalent value determined by the board, recent rounds of investor financing, or book value. Book value, however, may significantly understate the value of the company as an ongoing entity, especially if it has limited hard assets and/or shareholder equity. That means that if the company were sold or went public, the employees could get a windfall. Phantom stock is usually offered at no cost to the employee; thus, pricing is generally not an issue. A company that did require payment for phantom stock would have the same considerations as one issuing a Section 409A-compliant SAR.

Liquidity

Because SARs and phantom stock are essentially cash bonuses, companies need to figure out how to pay for them. Even if awards are paid out in shares (as in stock-settled SARs or RSUs), employees will want to sell the shares, at least in sufficient amounts to pay their taxes. In public companies that issue stock-settled awards, this is not a problem. The employee can simply sell the shares. In closely held companies, no matter how the award is settled, there needs to be a way to turn it into cash.

Companies can provide for this in a variety of ways. Some startup companies specify that the award will vest only if the company is sold or goes public (a company could vest the award before this, but that means the employee would have to pay taxes before there is a liquidity event). That means, however, that many employees will consider these awards to have little value if they view a liquidity event as an uncertain possibility or believe that they may not stay with the employer until one occurs. Because employees discount the value of awards with these conditions, companies would have to give larger awards to get the same degree of employee incentive.

If payout is not based on a liquidity event, some form of company funding is needed. The company can just make a promise to pay, but the employee may then view the award with some skepticism. What if the money isn't there when vesting occurs? To provide some certainty, the company can put cash aside as the award builds in value. This can be held in general reserves (subject to an excess accumulated earnings tax if the number becomes too large), but that would make the money available for any other business use. An alternative is to sequester the money in a "rabbi trust" (named for a ruling involving a rabbi), a deferred compensation arrangement in which funds are placed in a trust whose assets are available to creditors in the event of the company's insolvency. Because the trust's funds are subject to forfeiture in the event of insolvency, the beneficiary is not taxed until the award vests and is paid. Rules for the operation of rabbi trusts have become more specific, and such trusts should be established with the advice of qualified counsel. The company (not the employee) is taxed on any income from the trust, and the company cannot take a tax deduction for the funds until they are paid to the employee.

Accounting Issues

Phantom stock and cash-settled SARs are subject to liability accounting, meaning the accounting costs associated with them are not settled until they pay out or expire. For cash-settled SARs, the compensation expense for awards is estimated each quarter using an option-pricing model and then trued-up when the SAR is settled; for phantom stock, the underlying value is calculated each quarter and trued-up through the final settlement date. Phantom stock is treated in the same way as deferred cash compensation.

In contrast, if a SAR is settled in stock, then the accounting is the same as for an option. The company must record the fair value of the award at grant and recognize expense ratably over the expected service period. If the award is performance-vested, the company must estimate how long it will take to meet the goal. If the performance measurement is tied to the company's stock price, it must use an option-pricing model to determine when and if the goal will be met.

Accounting issues are covered in greater detail in this book's chapter on accounting.

Choosing a Plan

SARs generally make the most sense for companies that anticipate rapid share value increases or for startup companies whose stock has little initial value; phantom stock plans are more common in companies with more stable values.

To understand why this is so, imagine that a company is choosing between how many units of phantom stock to give out versus how many units of SARs. An appraisal firm would tell you that for every unit of a full-value award like phantom stock, you could give out two, three, or more units of SARs, depending on the prospects for your company and how volatile the stock price is. That's because the SAR has value only if the share price goes up, but phantom stock has value even if it goes down. It is the same as the difference between giving someone a share and giving someone an option that is valuable only if share prices increase. If most of the future value rests in appreciation, then the employee who is granted SARs may be giving up very little compared with one who is granted phantom stock. But in more mature companies, where there may be less appreciation, the SAR holder would be giving up a lot.

In companies with highly volatile stock, there is the risk that how much SARs holders get will be a result of the luck of the draw. Say a company's stock goes from $3 to $15 in the first year, from $15 to $6 in the year after that, from $6 back to $20 in year three, and $20 to $14 in year four. If employee A comes when stock is at $3, and it vests three years later at $20, he is very happy. If employee B comes along the next year when it is $15 and has options that vest in three years when it drops to $14, she is very unhappy. To mitigate this, it is better to give out smaller grants more frequently than to "front-load" awards on entry.

CHAPTER 5

ESOPs, Profit Sharing, and 401(k) Plans

COREY ROSEN

Employee stock ownership plans (ESOPs), tax-qualified profit sharing plans, and 401(k) plans can be very appealing ways to share ownership broadly with employees. All of these retirement plans offer the common benefit that corporate contributions are deductible when made to the plan but not taxed to the employee until the benefit is actually distributed (and even that can be delayed if a departing employee rolls the distribution into an IRA or other retirement account). No other compensation strategies allow employees to acquire a nonrestricted (in other words, fully vested) right to a benefit but not pay tax on it at the time, and no other strategies allow an employer a tax deduction before the employee pays ordinary income taxes.

Moreover, ESOPs in particular have a variety of additional tax benefits. ESOPs can borrow money, which the company can repay entirely in pre-tax dollars. Some company owners who sell their holdings to an ESOP can defer the gains made on the sale. Most dividends paid on ESOP shares are deductible. And, in S corporations, profits attributed to the ESOP's ownership are not taxable (so in 100% ESOP companies, no income taxes are due at the federal and, often, state level). Profit sharing plans and 401(k) plans do not have the same level of benefits but may be simpler to set up and maintain.

There is, however, a major constraint: these plans are governed by the Employee Retirement Income Security Act (ERISA). Passed in 1974 in the wake of pension scandals, the law was broadly drafted to cover a variety of employee benefits, including health insurance plans, pension plans, profit sharing plans, ESOPs, retirement savings plans, cafeteria plans, and other benefit plans meant to provide financial security to a broad group of employees. The basic idea is simple: the government provides employees and employers with tax breaks if their plans provide benefits on a nondiscriminatory basis across the work force. To do that, ERISA relies on several key concepts:

- *Operate the plan for the "exclusive benefit of plan participants."* Despite what it sounds like, a plan can benefit companies and other people as well, but when there is a conflict of interest, the interests of participants should prevail.

- *Govern the plan with an "eye sole" to the interests of participants.* ERISA plans are operated by plan trustees. Trustees can be anyone, including officers of the company. Some companies, however, hire independent professionals. Either way, a trustee is required by law to make sure the plan is operated primarily for the benefit of the people in it, not for the company or its owners. In an ESOP, this means, among other things, not overpaying for company stock.

- *Make prudent investment decisions for the plan.* Any funds in ERISA plans used for retirement should be invested in a way that a sensible, careful investor would invest them. Excess risk is discouraged, but so is parking all the money in a passbook savings account. There is a special exception for ESOPs, however. Here, ERISA not only permits but requires plans to be primarily invested in company stock, unless it is clear that that investment is in imminent danger of failing.

- *Broadly include those who work for the company and meet minimal requirements.* Generally, this means at a minimum all employees who have worked for at least 1,000 hours in a year must become eligible in the following year. There are some exceptions, however, such as employees covered by a bargaining agreement or employees in a separate line of business.[1]

---

1. There are also provisions that allow a company to exclude up to 30% of its non-highly compensated employees who otherwise meet the requirements,

- *Allocate benefits fairly.* Benefits can be allocated based on relative pay or a more level formula, but pay over $225,000 (in 2007) does not count.

- *Make benefits subject to vesting.* Most retirement plans allow companies to require that employees stay a certain amount of time before they earn any benefits contributed by the company.

- *Have a process for employees to contest decisions.* ERISA spells out a variety of specific procedures by which employees can argue that they were improperly denied benefits. The first level is to try to resolve the matter with the company. The second is to ask the government to step in (usually the U.S. Department of Labor [DOL], although the DOL's resources for this are limited). The third is to sue in federal courts.

- *Preserve the benefit in a trust for long-term wealth building.* All retirement plans governed by ERISA provide the employee with special tax benefits. Unlike other ownership arrangements discussed in this book, ownership through an ESOP is not taxed when the employee is vested in the benefit, but rather when it is received (which normally is some time much later, such as after the employee leaves the company). But employees usually have only a limited ability to take money out of the plan while still working (mostly in 401(k) plans through loans) and face a tax penalty if they don't put the money in an IRA or other retirement account when they actually get it after leaving the company.

In short, if you want the benefits of one of these plans, you have to meet a number of rules. You cannot pick and choose who you want to allow to be in the plan, nor can you base their awards on assessments of merit or adopt other discretionary approaches. If you can live with that, however, these plans are far more financially advantageous for the company and the employee than other approaches.

---

but it is extremely rare and usually impractical for ESOP companies to use this exception.

Employee Stock Ownership Plans (ESOPs)

In creating an ESOP, a company sets up an employee benefit trust, which it funds by contributing cash to buy company stock, contributing shares directly, or having the trust borrow money to buy stock, with the company making contributions to the plan to enable it to repay the loan. Generally, at least all full-time employees with a year or more of service are in the plan. To assure that these rules are met, ESOPs must appoint a trustee to act as the plan fiduciary. This can be anyone, although larger companies tend to appoint outside trust institutions, while smaller companies typically appoint managers or create ESOP trust committees. ESOPs are designed to invest primarily in the stock of the employer and can buy treasury shares, newly issued shares, or shares from exiting owners.

One very important point is widely misunderstood: employees almost never contribute to the plan; instead, contributions are funded by the company as a benefit, and shares are allocated to employee accounts on a nondiscriminatory basis, much as in a profit sharing plan. It's worth repeating that: *as a rule, employees do not buy shares in an ESOP.* Over the years, we have found that many people considering ESOPs have a difficult time understanding how that can be. The answer is simple: the company funds the plan.

An ESOP can be used for many purposes, including the following:

- The most common application is *to buy the shares of a departing owner of a closely held company.* In C corporations, owners can defer tax on the gains they have made from the sale to an ESOP if the ESOP holds 30% or more of the company's stock (and certain other requirements are met). Moreover, the purchase can be made in pretax corporate dollars.

- *To divest or acquire subsidiaries, buy back shares from the market, or restructure existing benefit plans* by replacing current benefit contributions with a leveraged ESOP.

- *To buy newly issued shares in the company, with the borrowed funds being used to buy new productive capital.* The company can, in effect, finance growth or acquisitions in pretax dollars while these same dollars create an employee benefit plan.

- *To simply be an employee benefit plan for companies that want to share ownership broadly.* In public companies especially, an ESOP contribution is often used as part or all of a match to employee deferrals to a 401(k) plan.

Funding

The most sophisticated use of an ESOP is to borrow money. The company borrows money from a lender and reloans it to the ESOP; the ESOP then uses the money to buy shares. The company makes tax-deductible contributions to the trust to enable it to repay the loan. This is called a "leveraged" ESOP. The company can also use dividends on the shares to repay the loan; these dividends become deductible to the company. In effect, the parallel loan structure allows the company to borrow money to acquire stock and, by funneling the loan through the ESOP, deduct both principal and interest. The company can use proceeds from the loan for any legitimate business purpose. Sellers to an ESOP can also be lenders. The stock is put into a "suspense account," where it is released to employee accounts as the loan is repaid.

The ESOP can also be funded directly by discretionary corporate contributions of cash that are used to buy existing shares or simply by the contribution of shares. These contributions to an ESOP are tax-deductible, generally up to 25% of the total eligible payroll of plan participants.

How Shares Get to Employees

The rules for ESOPs are similar to the rules for other tax-qualified ERISA plans in terms of participation, allocation, vesting, and distribution, but several special considerations apply.

All employees over age 21 who work for more than 1,000 hours in a plan year must be included in the next plan year (or earlier) unless they are covered by a collective bargaining unit (and the ESOP issue is negotiated in good faith), are in a separate line of business with at least 50 employees not covered by the ESOP, or fall into one of several limited anti-discrimination exemptions.

Shares are allocated to individual employee accounts based on relative compensation (generally, all W-2 compensation is counted), on a more level formula (such as per capita or by seniority), or on some combination of the two. The allocated shares are subject to vesting. If the plan provides for vesting all at once, called "cliff" vesting, employees must be 100% vested after three years of service; if vesting is gradual, it must not be slower than 20% after two years and 20% per year more until 100% is reached after six years. A faster vesting schedule applies where the ESOP contribution is used as a match to employee 401(k) deferrals.

When employees reach age 55 and have 10 years of participation in the plan, the company must either give them the option of diversifying 25% of their account balances among at least three other investment alternatives, or simply pay the amount out to the employees. At age 60 with 10 years of service, employees can have 50% diversified or distributed to them.

When employees retire, die, or become disabled, the company must distribute their vested shares to them or their beneficiaries no later than the last day of the plan year following the year of their departure. For employees leaving before reaching retirement age, distribution must begin no later than the last day of the sixth plan year following their year of separation from service. Payments can be in substantially equal installments out of the trust over five years, or they can be made in a lump sum. With the installment method, a company normally pays out a portion of the stock from the trust each year.

Closely held companies and some thinly traded public companies must repurchase the shares from departing employees at their fair market value, as determined by an independent appraiser. This so-called "put option" can be exercised by the employee in one of two 60-day periods, one starting when the employee receives the distribution and the second period one year after that. The employee can choose which one to use. This obligation should be considered at the outset of the ESOP and be factored into the company's ability to repay the loan.

Rules and Limitations

Shares in the plan are held in individual employee accounts. As contributions are made, they are allocated to each participant in the plan. In a leveraged ESOP, as the loan is repaid, these shares are released to the accounts of plan participants, based either on the principal paid or the percentage of total principal plus interest due that is paid that year. The amount *contributed* to repay the principal on the loan is what counts for determining if the company is within the limits for contributions allowed each year and for the purpose of calculating the tax deduction. The value of the shares released, however, is the amount used on the income statement, where it counts as a compensation cost.

Limitations on Contributions

Congress has been generous in providing tax benefits for ESOPs, but there are limits. Generally, companies can contribute and deduct up to 25% of the total eligible payroll of plan participants, whether contributed in the form of cash or stock or as a payment to cover the principal portion of an ESOP loan. Interest payments on a loan are deductible as interest. Eligible pay is essentially all the pay (including employee deferrals into benefit plans) of people actually in the plan up to $225,000 per participant (as of 2007; this and other dollar limits described here for defined contribution plans are indexed annually for inflation).

In C corporations, there are separate 25% limits for contributions to pay principal on ESOP loans and other contributions to the ESOP or to other plans; thus, a company with a leveraged ESOP and a profit sharing plan, for example, has a 50% total limit (up to 25% for a leveraged ESOP plus up to 25% for the profit sharing plan or any other defined contribution plan). However, in S corporations, company contributions to both leveraged ESOPs and other defined contribution plans all fall under a single 25%-of-pay calculation.

In C corporations, "reasonable" dividends paid on shares acquired by the ESOP can be used to repay an ESOP loan, and these are not included in the 25% of pay calculations. S corporations can use distributions on earnings to help repay the loan, although these are not deductible as they are in C corporations (but they are also not taxable to the ESOP). In S corporations, interest payments do count toward the 25% of eligible pay limits. In a leveraged ESOP in a C corporation, shares forfeited by employees who leave the company before they have fully vested rights to their shares are allocated to everyone else, but are not counted in the percentage limitations.

There are a number of limitations to these provisions, however. First, no one ESOP participant can get a contribution of more than 100% of pay in any year from the principal payments on the loan or from the direct ESOP contributions made that year that are attributable to that employee, or more than $45,000 (as of 2007), whichever is less. In figuring payroll, pay over $225,000 per year (as of 2007) does not count toward total contribution limits. Second, the company's other qualified benefit plans must be taken into account when assessing this limit. This means that employee deferrals into 401(k) plans, as well as other employer contributions to 401(k), stock bonus, or profit sharing plans, are added to the ESOP contribution and cannot exceed 100% of pay or $45,000 (as of 2007) in any year. Third, the interest on an ESOP loan repayment in a C corporation is excludable from the 25%-of-pay individual limit only if no more than one-third of the benefits are allocated to highly compensated employees, as defined by Internal Revenue Code Section 414(q). If the one-third rule is not met, forfeitures are also counted in determining how much an employee is getting each year.

Voting

In private companies, employees must be able to direct the trustee as to the voting of shares *allocated* to their accounts on several key issues, including closing, sale, liquidation, recapitalization, and other issues having to do with the basic structure of the company. They do not, however, have to be able to vote for the board of directors or on other typical corporate governance issues, although companies can voluntarily provide these rights. Instead, the plan trustee votes the shares, usually at the direction of management. In public companies, employees must be able to vote on all issues.

What these rules mean is that governance is not really an issue for ESOP companies unless they want it to be. If companies want employees to have only the most limited role in corporate governance, they can; if they want to go beyond this, they can as well. In practice, companies that do provide employees with a substantial governance role find that it does not result in dramatic changes in the way the company is run.

Finally, in private companies and some thinly traded public companies, all ESOP transactions must be based on a current appraisal by an independent, outside valuation expert.

Tax Benefits to the Selling Shareholder

One of the major benefits of an ESOP for closely held C corporations is found in Section 1042 of the Internal Revenue Code. Under it, a seller to an ESOP may be able to qualify for a deferral of taxation on the gain made from the sale. Several requirements apply, the most significant of which are:

1. The seller must have held the stock for three years before the sale.
2. The stock must not have been acquired through stock options or other employee benefit plans.
3. The ESOP must own 30% or more of the value of the company's shares and must continue to hold this amount for three years unless the company is sold. Shares the company repurchases from departing employees do not count. Stock sold in a transaction that brings the ESOP to 30% of the total shares qualifies for the deferral treatment.
4. Shares qualifying for the deferral cannot be allocated to the accounts of the selling shareholders; to lineal descendants, brothers or sisters, spouses, or parents of the selling shareholders; or to any more-than-25% shareholders.

If these rules are met, the seller (or sellers) can take the proceeds from the sale and reinvest them in "qualified replacement property" during the period running from three months before to twelve months after the sale and defer any capital gains tax until these new investments are sold. Qualified replacement property essentially means stocks, bonds, warrants, or debentures of domestic corporations receiving not more than 25% of their income from passive investment. Mutual funds and real estate trusts do not qualify. If the replacement securities are held until death, they are subject to a step-up in basis at that time, so capital gains taxes would never be paid.

Very often, lenders ask for replacement securities as part or all of the collateral for an ESOP loan. This strategy may be beneficial to sellers who are selling only part of their holdings because it frees up the corporation to use its assets for other borrowing and could enhance the future value of the company.

Corporate Tax Benefits

As noted above, companies can use ESOPs to borrow money and repay the loan entirely in pretax dollars. In addition, companies can take a tax deduction for reasonable dividends that are used to repay a loan, that are passed through directly to employees, or that employees voluntarily reinvest in company stock. Contributions not used to repay an ESOP loan are tax-deductible as well, even if made in the form of treasury or new shares.

ESOPs in S Corporations

ESOPs can own stock in S corporations. While these ESOPs operate under most of the same rules as they do in C corporations, there are important differences. As noted above, interest payments on S corporation ESOP loans count toward the contribution limits (they normally do not in C companies). Dividends (i.e., S corporation "distributions") paid on ESOP shares are also not deductible. Most important, sellers to an ESOP in an S corporation do not qualify for the tax-deferred Section 1042 rollover treatment.

On the other hand, the ESOP is unique among S corporation owners in that it does not have to pay federal income tax on any profits attributable to it (state rules vary). This can make an ESOP very attractive in some cases. It also makes converting to an S corporation very appealing when a C corporation's ESOP owns a high percentage of the company's stock.

For owners who want to use an ESOP to provide a market for their shares, generally it will make sense to convert to C status before setting up an ESOP. Where selling shares is not a priority, or where the seller either does not have substantial capital gains taxes due on the sale or has other reasons to prefer staying an S corporation, an S corporation ESOP can provide significant tax benefits. However, keep in mind that any distributions paid to owners must be paid pro-rata to the ESOP. The ESOP can use these distributions to purchase additional shares, to build up cash for future repurchases of employee shares, or just to add to employee accounts.

While the S corporation rules make ESOPs very attractive, legislation passed in 2001 makes it clear that companies may not create ESOPs primarily to benefit a few people. For instance, some accountants were promoting plans in which a company would set up an S corporation management company owned by just a few people that would manage a large C corporation. The C corporation's profits would flow through the S corporation's ESOP and thus not be taxed.

The rules Congress enacted are complicated, but they boil down to two essential points. First, people who own more than 10% of the allocated shares in the ESOP, or who own 20% counting their family members, are considered "disqualified" persons. The ESOP's ownership is defined to include synthetic equity, such as options, phantom stock, and most kinds of deferred compensation, even though these are generally held outside of the ESOP. Second, if these disqualified people together own 50% or more of the company's shares (counting their synthetic equity), then they cannot get allocations in the ESOP without extraordinary tax penalties. Congress also directed the IRS to apply this onerous tax treatment to any plan it deems to be substantially for the purpose of evading taxes rather than providing employee benefits.

Financial Issues for Employees

When an employee receives a distribution from the plan, it is taxable unless rolled over into an IRA or other qualified account.

Otherwise, the amounts contributed by the employer are taxable as ordinary income, while any appreciation on the shares is taxable as capital gains. In addition, if the employee receives the distribution before normal retirement age and does not roll over the funds, a 10% excise tax is added.

While the stock is in the plan, however, it is not taxable to employees. It is rare, moreover, for employees to give up wages to participate in an ESOP or to purchase stock directly through a plan (this raises difficult securities law issues for closely held firms). Most ESOPs either are in addition to existing benefit plans or replace other defined contribution plans, usually at a higher contribution level.

Accounting

In nonleveraged plans, the contribution to the ESOP shows up directly as a compensation cost. In leveraged plans, the principal payments and dividend payments on unallocated shares that are used to repay a loan show up as a compensation charge as well; dividends on allocated shares show up as a charge to retained earnings. The debt of the ESOP shows up as corporate debt, with an offsetting contra equity account that is reduced as the loan is repaid.

Profit Sharing Plans

Tax-qualified profit sharing plans[2] are similar to ESOPs in many ways. The rules for eligibility, vesting, and distribution are generally the same, but there is no diversification requirement at age 55 in private company profit sharing plans. Public companies often combine profit sharing plans with 401(k) plans and are subject to the very strict diversification requirements described in the section on 401(k) plans below. Companies can postpone distributions until retirement age, but they must keep the employee's account invested in prudent investments in the period between termination and retire-

---

2.   Qualified profit sharing plans are different from bonuses paid directly to employees based on profits. These are taxed like wage compensation.

ment. Companies cannot use a profit sharing plan to borrow money to buy company stock, sellers cannot get tax deferrals on sales to a profit sharing plan, dividends paid on stock in the plan cannot be deducted, and in an S corporation, the profit sharing plan must pay unrelated business income tax at the highest personal income tax rates on its ownership of shares in the corporation. The plan cannot use its assets to pay these taxes, so additional cash contributions from the company are required. Essentially, the only real tax benefit of a profit sharing plan investing in employer stock is the basic one we described at the outset of this chapter: companies can deduct contributions when they are made, but employees do not pay taxes until they receive the cash out of the plan or the successor account they roll the distribution into. Valuations of stock are not a statutory requirement but are an essential practical one. Employees do not have any required voting rights on shares in their plans.

A profit sharing plan can invest primarily in employer stock, but these plans are subject to stricter fiduciary standards than ESOPs concerning employer stock. The presumption is that they should be more diversified. Companies can help overcome this presumption somewhat by writing into plan documents that the plan is intended to be primarily invested in employer stock, but the courts have come to mixed conclusions on just how much protection this provides.

So why use a profit sharing plan instead of an ESOP? Companies that do not need the special ESOP tax benefits will find profit sharing plans both less complicated and more flexible, particularly in terms of distributions. Companies can contribute cash or stock to fund the plan. Despite their name, profit sharing plans no longer have to receive distributions of actual profits. Companies can fund plans without any reference to profitability. But companies using these plans should be sure to have an independent valuation and a trustee whose decisions will be seen as both independent and in the best interests of plan participants. Especially in closely held companies, profit sharing plans have only occasionally been used as a primary employee ownership vehicle.

For accounting purposes, employer contributions to profit sharing plans are counted as compensation.

401(k) Plans

Company stock is a common component of 401(k) plans in public companies and, occasionally, closely held companies. Several factors favor the use of a 401(k) plan as a vehicle for employee ownership in public companies. From the company's perspective, its own stock may be one of the most cost-effective means of matching employee contributions. If there are existing treasury shares or the company issues new shares, contributing them to the 401(k) plan may impose no immediate cash cost on the company; in fact, it would provide a tax deduction. Other shareholders would suffer dilution, of course. If the company has to buy shares to fund the match, at least the dollars are being used to invest in the company itself rather than something else. From the employees' standpoint, company stock is the investment they know best and so may be attractive to people who either do not want to spend the time to learn about alternatives or have a strong belief in their own company. Balanced against these advantages, of course, must be an appreciation on both the part of the employee and the company that a failure to diversify a retirement portfolio is very risky.

For closely held companies, 401(k) plans are less appealing, although they are very appropriate in some cases. If employees are given an option to buy company stock, this will trigger securities law issues most private firms want to avoid.[3] Employer matches make more sense, but they require the company to either dilute ownership or reacquire shares from selling shareholders. In many closely held businesses, diluting ownership may be undesirable for control reasons, and reacquiring shares may be impractical because there may be no sellers. Moreover, the 401(k) approach does not provide the Section 1042 "rollover" tax benefit that selling to an ESOP in a C corporation does, and the maximum amount that can be contributed is usually (although it does not have to be) a function of how much employees put into savings. That will limit how much an employer can actually buy from a seller through a 401(k) plan to a fraction of what the ESOP can buy. In S corporations, 401(k) plan

---

3. Details on this issue are in the chapter on securities laws.

contributions in company stock are subject to the same unfavorable tax treatment as contributions to profit sharing plans.

Despite these limitations, 401(k) plans are attractive as ownership vehicles where a company wants employees to become owners but has no need to buy out existing owners or use the borrowing features of an ESOP. A company can simply match employee deferrals with company stock or make a straight percentage-of-pay contribution to all employees eligible to be in the plan in the form of company stock. ESOPs can also be part of a 401(k) plan, either formally or informally. The ESOP contribution can be considered the match to employee deferrals in either case.

If using a 401(k) plan, however, it is important to be especially vigilant about fiduciary issues. In the wake of Enron, WorldCom, and other disasters, several dozen lawsuits were filed, almost all in public companies, against boards, officers, trustees, plan committee members, and anyone else associated with 401(k) plans that were invested in company stock that declined sharply. As a result, in 2006 Congress limited companies' ability to force employees to hold company stock in their 401(k) and other defined contribution plan accounts. Companies can no longer force employees to hold company stock purchased with their own contributions and, furthermore, must allow employees to diversify out of any company stock that their employer has contributed to their accounts after three years of service. (These new rules do not apply to ESOPs unless they are in public companies and are combined with a 401(k) plan.)

The post-Enron lawsuits focused on a variety of issues, such as whether fiduciaries should have removed company stock as an investment choice, should not have promoted company stock as a deferral choice if they knew it was risky, should have stopped making contributions in stock, should have allowed employees more flexibility to diversify company stock in their accounts, should have released information not already public about impending financial problems, and other issues. Court decisions on these trials have been mixed. Where 401(k) plans had ESOP components requiring investment in company stock, the courts have tended to side with the companies unless there was evidence that fiduciaries knew or should have known the stock was going to fall sharply. Otherwise, courts have generally looked to see if fiduciaries had reason to believe that the investment was a reasonable choice at any particular time. Where there was inside information that the stock price was about to be in trouble, courts have generally sided with plaintiffs, ruling that employers should have disclosed that (even if this caused securities laws problems in public companies). Courts have taken a fairly expansive view as well about who is a fiduciary, including not only anyone who served in that capacity but also those who caused decisions to be made or who were responsible for monitoring the activities of fiduciaries who acted improperly.

Given this developing area of law, advisors are generally urging clients with company stock in 401(k) plans to use independent fiduciaries, allow for diversification after a reasonable time (in public companies, at least), and consider putting an upper limit on the percentage of an employee's account that can be held in employer stock. In closely held companies, 401(k) plans should be funded by the employer rather than by employee deferrals, except in very unusual circumstances (such as when employees are trying to buy a company whose sale cannot otherwise be financed; even then extreme care is needed to design a plan effectively).

The accounting treatment of 401(k) plans is straightforward; any corporate contributions are charged to earnings, while employee purchases of shares add to shareholder capital.

CHAPTER 6

Deferred Compensation Issues

COREY ROSEN

In theory, compensation should be taxable at the point when an employee has an irrevocable right to it, whether it is actually paid or not. Employees can choose to defer compensation—and its taxation—if there is a significant risk that the right to it will be forfeited. For example, if the money the company sets aside (literally or just by recording an obligation to pay) is available to claims from creditors, the IRS will consider the award to be subject to a "substantial risk of forfeiture." But by the early 2000s, more and more stories came out about perceived abuses of deferred compensation by top executives in large companies. Over the years, companies had developed many techniques for using trusts and similar vehicles to all but guarantee deferred compensation payments, while still adhering to the technical rules exempting such funds from immediate taxation to the executive. In effect, these techniques provided executives with interest-free loans of the tax money that would otherwise have been due, postponed the company's tax deduction until the compensation was actually paid, and meant the assets were unavailable to the company in the interim. In the most high-profile cases, such as Enron, executives were able to collect large amounts of deferred compensation owed to them just before their companies collapsed.

Until 2004, IRS rules for the tax treatment of compensation deferred beyond its due date were unsettled. Could an employee choose to defer compensation to any time in the future at any point before the award's scheduled payout without any tax consequences for the employee or company? Most lawyers thought not and advised clients to require advance notification of several months or more. But others disagreed, and practices varied widely.

In response to all this, in the American Jobs Creation Act of 2004, Congress added new Section 409A to the Internal Revenue Code (the Code), adopting sweeping changes to the tax treatment of deferred compensation that impose steep taxes and penalties on the recipients of awards that do not comply with the new rules. Service providers' total deferrals under a nonqualified deferred compensation plan (NDCP) that does not adhere to these rules are immediately taxed as income at vesting, and the holder is assessed a 20% penalty on the amount of the deferral and any earnings attributable to it, plus cumulative interest at the underpayment rate plus 1% on the tax that should have been paid on the original deferral and any related earnings. "Service provider" includes employees as well as other people providing services to a company who receive compensation for their time.

Under this new law, the halcyon days of discretionary deferrals are essentially over. As of January 1, 2005, any compensation deferred under an NDCP is currently taxable unless it is subject to a substantial risk of forfeiture[1] or satisfies the rigorous requirements of Section 409A. For purposes of Section 409A, nonqualified deferred compensation generally does *not* include: (1) qualified benefit plans, such as ESOPs or 401(k) plans; (2) sick leave, death benefits, or similar arrangements; (3) statutory stock options (i.e., ISOs and ESPPs qualified under Section 423 of the Code); (4) NSOs granted at fair market value (subject to certain limitations); (5) restricted stock awards; and (6) non-discounted SARs that meet other requirements. All other forms of nonqualified deferred compensation can be assumed to be deferred under a NDCP, *including:* (1) nonqualified ESPPs that include a discount feature; (2) NSOs that include a deferral feature (i.e., allowing an employee to defer receipt of the award after it has already been exercised); and (3) phantom stock, RSUs, performance shares, and similar vehicles.

The IRS issued transition guidance on Section 409A in Notice 2005-1 (December 2004, as revised in January 2005); and followed

---

1.   Using the principles of Section 83 of the Code.

with final regulations in April 2007. The final regulations become effective on January 1, 2009, although companies must operate their plans in good-faith compliance with either the proposed or final regulations before that deadline. Awards granted before the effective date of the law can be brought into compliance until January 1, 2009.

The new tax rules will strike many companies and their executives as onerous, confusing, and unnecessary. It is, however, entirely possible to establish reasonable deferred compensation programs that fall clearly within what the law allows. There are three key elements to this strategy:

1. Use equity compensation arrangements that are exempt from the law.

2. Structure non-exempt deferred equity compensation to comply with the law, for example by providing that awards will not pay out until after a major event, such as termination, retirement, change of control, death, or unforeseen emergency (a term defined in the law that could include long-term disability or personal bankruptcy). The plan can pay out sooner if the employee or employer simply specifies the time to which payment will be deferred well in advance or if the payout is made no later than two and a half months into the year after the year of vesting. What employees are giving up here is the ability to choose to defer income to an unspecified future date that can be chosen at their discretion any time before the actual payout.

3. Use non-equity deferred compensation plans exempted from the requirements. These include tax-qualified retirement plans, such as 401(k) plans, ESOPs, profit sharing plans, and pension plans; tax-sheltered annuity plans; legitimate vacation leave, sick days, disability and/or death benefits, and compensatory time; and special medical savings plans, such as HSAs.

This chapter focuses on the equity compensation aspects of deferred compensation. For the most part, it should not be difficult to design the kind of packages you want, provided you follow a few basic rules.

Specific Application of the New Rules to Equity Awards

As we have noted, many equity and equity-based awards are exempted from the Section 409A definition of NDCP, either as a result of the statutory language or under the regulatory guidance described below. Note that awards granted before October 3, 2004, that were earned and vested as of December 31, 2004, are exempt from Section 409A regardless of their terms (so long as such terms are not materially modified after October 3, 2004). In September 2005, the IRS issued proposed regulations under 409A, with further elaboration in Notice 2006-4, which was actually issued in 2005. Those proposed regulations will be superseded by the final regulations, which go into effect on January 1, 2009. The final regulations are almost 400 pages long and cover all aspects of 409A, not just those dealing with equity compensation. This chapter does not provide a summary of that other material.

General Application of the New Rules

If compensation deferred under an NDCP is not otherwise subject to a substantial risk of forfeiture, it will be taxed at the time of vesting unless the following conditions are satisfied:

1. The initial election to defer (including form of payment) is made before the start of the year in which the compensation is earned. An election to defer "performance-based" compensation may be made up to six months before the end of the performance period.

2. Any elections to further defer a payment must be made at least twelve months before the date the deferred compensation would otherwise have been received, and in most cases deferral must be for at least five years after the original payment date.

3. Distributions may be permitted only upon separation from service (for certain "key employees" of public companies, generally the company's 50 highest-paid officers, this includes a six-month waiting period); at a specified date or dates (under

a fixed schedule); or upon disability, death, change in control, or unforeseeable emergency, in each case as such terms are defined by Section 409A and its regulations.

4. No acceleration of payments is permissible, except for limited circumstances in which accelerations are nondiscretionary. For example, a payment can be accelerated to comply with a domestic relations order issued pursuant to a divorce.

Note that short-term deferrals in which the payment is made no later than two and one-half months after the close of the year the substantial risk of forfeiture lapses will not run afoul of Section 409A.

NSOs and SARs

The Section 409A rules exempt NSOs and SARs ("stock rights") for which: (1) the exercise price can never be less than the fair market value of the underlying stock on the date of grant; (2) the stock right is exercisable for "service recipient" stock; (3) the stock right includes no deferral features other than deferral of income until exercise; and (4) the stock right is not modified in a way that would otherwise subject it to Section 409A. In addition, for SARs, the number of shares subject to the grant must be fixed on the grant date, and the payment amount cannot exceed the stock's appreciation between the grant date and exercise date.

An employer that does not want to abide by these rules for SARs can design a SAR award to comply with Section 409A. In that case, the employer can determine the number of shares subject to the award some time after the grant date or use an informal valuation method for setting the exercise price, but it must specify a payout date or event instead of allowing the employee to choose when to exercise.

As with the other exempt forms of compensation, stock rights may be thrown into the purview of Section 409A if they are coupled with features that would otherwise be classified as payments under an NDCP. For example, the payment of accrued dividends upon exercise is considered to be tantamount to a discount from fair market value and thus would subject the holder of a stock option or 409A-exempt SAR to the law's penalties. A separate payment of the equivalent amount can avoid this treatment, but that payment itself would be subject to the payment scheduling rules described above. Note that generally, stock rights transferred in a merger or acquisition will not trigger deferred compensation treatment if they comply with the 2004 regulations governing transfers of statutory options in a corporate transaction.

For purposes of setting the exercise price for exempt awards, Section 409A provides that fair market value may be determined using "any reasonable valuation method," and the regulations elaborate on this concept. With publicly traded companies, this is never a problem. However, with the stakes now raised for stock rights, privately held companies must pay special attention to the hurdles inherent in setting fair market value so as to avoid inadvertently granting NSOs or SARs at a discount. This is discussed in more detail below.

Restricted Stock and RSUs

Generally, grants of restricted stock (whether or not vested at grant) will be subject to Section 83 of the Code rather than to Section 409A (Section 83 covers most forms of individual equity compensation; its requirements are discussed in the chapter on restricted stock). However, the Section 409A rules note that a plan under which a service provider obtains a legally binding right to receive property in a future year may provide for the deferral of compensation and thus become an NDCP. An RSU, for example, will fall into Section 409A and accordingly must satisfy the general requirements to avoid early taxation. In practice, this means the payout must either be made immediately upon vesting, which is common, or be subject to a valid deferral election that meets the timing requirements described above.

Modifications

If an award's terms are changed to offer an additional deferral feature—such as an extension of the time to exercise—the award becomes subject to Section 409A.[2] In contrast, plan changes that allow different forms of payment, such as the addition of a cashless exercise feature, do not constitute modifications that make an award subject to Section 409A (although they may be considered modifications for other purposes, such as compliance with the tax rules governing ISOs).

Companies could bring discounted stock options or SARs that were not fully vested as of the end of 2004 into compliance with Section 409A up to the end of 2006 by replacing them with non-discounted stock options or SARs or by imposing a fixed exercise date or dates or allowing the optionee to choose a fixed date or dates.

Business Combinations

The option issuer may own as little as 20% of the service recipient company so long as the use of that company's stock has a legitimate business purpose. If a service provider works for a closely held subsidiary of a public company, only the public company's stock is the service recipient stock.

Performance Vesting

Stock options and SARs subject to Section 409A may vest based on performance criteria as long as the performance period is at least one year and the compensation is based solely on appreciation of the value of the stock. The performance criteria can be determined up to 90 days after the grant. Criteria can be subjective, but the more specific they are, the less likely they are to run afoul of the rules.

Valuation Requirements for Options and SARs

To avoid coverage under the Section 409A rules, valuations for SARs and NSOs in closely held companies need to adhere to more

---

2. The final regulations contain a limited exception for extensions of a stock right's exercise period upon separation from service and allow companies to extend the exercise period of a stock right that is "underwater," meaning the current fair market value is lower than the award's exercise price.

rigorous standards than have previously been the norm. Public companies can use the first or last trading price on the day the grant is awarded, the closing price from the day before the grant, or the mean of the high and low prices on the day before or day of the grant. They can also use the average stock price over the 30 days before or after the grant date as long as an irrevocable commitment to grant the right is made before the averaging period begins. Other reasonable methods are also acceptable. Closely held companies, however, must follow stricter rules.

The Section 409A regulations set forth three alternatives for closely held companies. Such issuers have a choice of:

- following the established standards for ESOP valuations, including hiring an outside appraiser;

- using a formula valuation that establishes fair market valuation for purposes of Treas. Reg. § 1.83-5 *and* that is used on a consistent basis for other transactions;

- using a price at which any recent equity sales were made in an arm's-length transaction; or

- if in business less than 10 years, using a formula valuation that meets somewhat (but not much) less rigorous guidelines.

The valuation method for grant and exercise can be different, but companies must be consistent in the methods they use for each. If a company uses recent sales of equity for grant valuations in 2007, it cannot use some other method in 2009, for instance.

ESOP Valuation Standards

Under the new rules, companies with ESOPs may simply use their existing valuations. Companies without ESOPs, however, may also consider adopting the ESOP company approach. ESOP rules require that an independent, outside appraisal be performed at least annually. The appraiser must be a qualified professional with no other business relationship to the company. The appraisals must determine what a willing buyer would pay a willing seller for the company. Specific rules were never adopted on how to conduct an appraisal, but a consensus has developed in the industry that asset value, comparable companies, and (usually most importantly) capitalization of future earnings should all be weighed. Once an enterprise value is established, appropriate discounts for whether the securities represent a control interest and a lack of marketability must be applied.

Treasury Regulations Section 1.83-5 Formula Valuations

Treas. Reg. § 1.83-5 sets out rules for setting the value of property subject to a "nonlapse restriction," i.e., a restriction on the acquisition or sale of the property that is not subject to subsequent change,[3] as follows:

> If stock in a corporation is subject to a nonlapse restriction which requires the transferee to sell such stock only at a formula price based on book value, a reasonable multiple of earnings or a reasonable combination thereof, the price so determined will ordinarily be regarded as determinative of the fair market value of such property for purposes of section 83. However, in certain circumstances the formula price will not be considered to be the fair market value of property subject to such a formula price restriction, even though the formula price restriction is a substantial factor in determining such value. For example, where the formula price is the current book value of stock, the book value of the stock at some time in the future may be a more accurate measure of the value of the stock than the current book value of the stock for purposes of determining the fair market value of the stock at the time the stock becomes substantially vested.

In other words, the formula must be more than formulaic—it must consider what approach most closely resembles reasonable fair market value. The Section 409A rules add to this the requirement that the same formula must be used for any nonlapse restrictions applicable to the transfer of shares of that class, and that that it be used for any noncompensatory purpose involving that class of stock, such as regulatory filings, loan covenants, issuances and repurchases

---

3.   Such as an NSO with time-based vesting that is subsequently modified, making it a new grant for Section 409A purposes.

of stock from non-service providers, and so on. This rule does not apply if the award is paid in stock and the stock is transferable without a nonlapse restriction. A key element here is that if the safe harbor is satisfied, the burden of proof is on the IRS to show the valuation method is unreasonable, rather than on the company to show the method is reasonable.

Start-Up Company Valuations

Issuers in business for less than 10 years are eligible to use a written valuation made "reasonably and in good faith" that takes into account relevant business factors and is performed by "a person or persons with significant knowledge and experience or training in performing significant valuations." The company must not reasonably anticipate a change of control in the next 90 days or IPO in the next 180 days and must have no class of tradable securities. The company's stock must not be subject to any put or call right.

General Issues in Determining Reasonableness

Any valuation needs to consider at least several factors, including the present value of future cash flows; asset value; comparable company valuations and relevant ratios (such as price to earnings); any prior sales of stock; consistent application of the value, premiums, and discounts for factors such as control, lack of marketability, and so on; and the relevance of other valuations performed for different purposes. Valuations that do not use information from the prior 12 months are not considered reasonable.

In guidance issued in Notice 2006-4, the IRS announced that as an interim measure under Section 409A, issuers could adopt any reasonable method for establishing fair market value for awards issued before January 1, 2005. For awards issued after that date, but before January 1, 2009, issuers can rely on the guidance in the proposed or final regulations.

CHAPTER 7

Accounting for Equity Compensation

PAM CHERNOFF

Equity compensation awards are treated as an expense on a company's income statement. In the past, it was possible to design stock option awards and employee stock purchase plans so that they did not lead to an accounting expense, even though other kinds of equity awards did. Companies could get by just putting their fair value in a footnote. But those days ended with the 2005 and 2006 implementation of a new equity compensation accounting standard.

Under the previous accounting standard, Accounting Principles Board Opinion No. 25, only stock options that had an exercise price equal to the grant date fair market value and vested over time and Section 423 employee stock purchase plan (ESPP) shares were eligible for favorable accounting treatment.[1] Other forms of equity compensation did result in an expense. Thus, many companies chose stock options over other types of awards.

However, under Statement of Financial Accounting Standards 123 (revised 2004) (FAS 123(R)), stock options no longer enjoy preferential treatment, meaning other types of awards are no longer at the competitive disadvantage that they were in the past, at least in terms of accounting. The accounting treatment of Section 423 ESPPs also has been revised, as discussed later in this chapter.

The thrust behind the accounting reforms was to give shareholders a better idea of just how much different kinds of equity awards

---

1. Section 423 is the Internal Revenue Code section that provides for certain tax incentives for employees participating in qualifying stock purchase plans.

would actually cost them. The Financial Accounting Standards Board (FASB), which is the private-sector body that sets U.S. accounting standards, wanted this to show up on the income statement, just as other compensation does. This was a controversial project that took many years to complete. Many companies argued that options have no cost to the company (they contended the cost is borne by shareholders in the form of dilution) or are a balance sheet, not income statement, issue. FASB prevailed, however.

The trick was now to figure out a way to assess a current value for awards whose total value (if any) would only be realized over time. That requires many assumptions and formulas, but the core idea is simple: What would someone actually pay today for an award with the same characteristics? It is important to understand that the changes in accounting have not changed the actual costs companies have always incurred with equity awards. They only change how and when shareholders see them, and how companies account for these costs in their financial statements.

Accounting issues are a concern for public companies or closely held companies that plan on an IPO. Other closely held companies must make sure they deal with accounting properly, but they do not want accounting expenses to drive program design, an outlook we at the NCEO strongly argue is appropriate.

This chapter provides a broad overview of accounting for equity compensation vehicles. Those who need an in-depth explanation of equity compensation accounting should refer to the NCEO book *Accounting for Equity Compensation* and, as always, consult with an accounting professional.

Cash-Settled vs. Stock-Settled Awards

FAS 123(R) treats awards that pay out (or "settle") in stock differently than awards that pay out in cash. For those that settle in stock, the company must determine the fair value of the award on the grant date and recognize that amount, meaning record it on its books, over the service period, which generally is the vesting period. If the award is made in the form of stock options or SARs, the company must use an option-pricing model to determine the fair value of the award. "Fair value" means how much the award itself, with all caveats and requirements (such as the expected amount of time until the option is exercised, any consideration that must be paid for it at grant, etc.) is worth at the time of grant. Theoretically, it is what an option or other award would sell for at grant if there were a large, open market for it, as there is, for instance, for options in commodity futures. The fair value as calculated at grant does not change during the life of the award even if the assumptions used in the option-pricing model turn out to be incorrect. Once the fair value is determined, companies can estimate the percentage of awards they believe will actually vest and recognize only that portion of the fair value. As time goes on, however, the company must adjust the expense recognized for actual forfeitures. For instance, if a company assumed at the outset that 20% of a grant would never vest, but it turned out that 30% never vested, the company would ultimately recognize only 70% of the grant's fair value.

In contrast, the expense for cash-settled awards is not determined with finality until the award is settled. Between the grant date and the settlement date, the company must make periodic estimates of the award's value for accounting purposes and recognize the expense over the remaining service period. Private companies can choose whether to do this by recognizing the award's intrinsic value (the difference between the exercise price and the stock's fair market value on the reporting date) or fair value in the reporting periods before the award is settled.

Table 9-1 gives an overview of the accounting rules that apply to varying types of equity compensation.

Option-Pricing Models

The "fair value" arrived at through an option-pricing model is distinct from "fair market value," which is the price a willing buyer would pay a willing seller for the underlying stock (as opposed to the option itself) in an arm's-length transaction. FAS 123(R) requires that option-pricing models used to determine an equity award's fair value include:

Table 9-1

Award Type	Accounting Treatment
Stock options and stock-settled SARs (time-based vesting)	Fair value determined at grant date and expensed over service period.
Stock options and stock-settled SARs (performance-based vesting)	Fair value determined at grant date and expensed over expected vesting period.
Section 423 ESPPs	Result in expense if discount greater than 5% or if plan includes a look-back feature. Expense recognized over offering period.
Restricted stock (granted at no cost to employee) and restricted stock units (RSUs)	Fair market value of award on grant date expensed over vesting period.
Restricted stock (employee pays for part or all of the cost at grant)	Intrinsic value of award on grant date (fair market value minus any consideration paid for it) expensed over vesting period.
Cash-settled SARs	Expense estimated and recognized over life of award. Fair value determined upon settlement or expiration.
Phantom stock	Expense estimated and recognized over life of award. Ultimate value that must be expensed determined only upon settlement or expiration.

- *The award's exercise price.*

- *The underlying stock's fair market value:* For public companies, this is the price for which the stock is trading on an exchange. For private companies, the board sets the fair market value. For tax reasons, this should be set using standards laid out in Internal Revenue Code Section 409A, which is discussed in detail in the chapter on deferred compensation.

- *The award's expected term:* Companies are allowed to project the average amount of time options will remain unexercised. This is generally shorter than the awards' contractual terms.

- *The underlying stock's expected volatility:* Private companies that cannot produce a reliable estimate of their stock volatility can look at similar public companies or industry indexes.

- *The underlying stock's expected dividend yield.*

- *The risk-free interest rate:* Generally the current Treasury rate applying to bills or bonds with terms equal to the award's expected term.

The accounting standard does not require the use of any particular model. In fact, it gives broad leeway for companies to choose which kind of model they wish to use. Historically, companies have relied on the Black-Scholes option-pricing model, which has the advantage of being clearly defined and broadly available. Black-Scholes was developed to price noncompensatory stock options that are traded on an exchange. People can buy options on all kinds of things—pork belly futures are the common example used. These options, which provide rights to acquire underlying shares or other rights, typically last a relatively short period of time (often a year or less) and can be traded freely, but they are generally not exercisable before their expiration date. You can sell your option in pork belly futures to someone else before it is exercised. For these reasons, Black-Scholes has been criticized as a method for valuing employee stock options, which typically have longer terms, are subject to vesting, and can be exercised at various times before expiration. Despite these concerns, many companies use this formula, and it has produced results that have not been greatly at variance with other models.

However, some companies find they need more flexibility than Black-Scholes allows. One possibility for those companies is to adopt a lattice model, a statistical technique that creates a tree of possible events. For example, in a binomial model, two possibilities are projected for each possible occurrence. The fair value is then arrived at by considering all of the possibilities, giving a greater weight to the more probable outcomes. Lattice models require a large amount of data and analysis; thus, they are generally practical only for public companies whose equity-compensation-related expense is quite large.

Equity Compensation Vehicles

Stock Options and Stock-Settled SARs with Time-Based Vesting

The accounting for stock options and stock-settled SARs that vest based only on time is relatively straightforward. The company uses an option-pricing model to determine the awards' fair value on the grant date and recognizes that cost over the vesting period. The inputs into the option-pricing model must include all of the six factors listed above.

The amount ultimately expensed may be adjusted to reflect actual forfeitures of awards that never vest. This adjustment is not an input into the model; rather, it is an adjustment to the fair value initially calculated using the option-pricing model. Note that only awards that never vest are treated as having been forfeited. The expense for awards that expire unexercised cannot be reversed.

Stock Options with Performance Vesting

The accounting for options and SARs that vest based on performance is similar to those that vest based on time. As long as the goal is not related to movements in stock price, then the company estimates when it expects the goal to be met and recognizes the compensation cost over the expected vesting period. Thus, the model inputs for expected term and possibly interest rate and dividend yield will be different, but the other inputs will likely stay the same. However, if the performance goal is a target price for company stock, the company must use an option-pricing model to determine when and if that goal is likely to be met and incorporate that estimate into its assumptions.

The expense for options that vest based on performance goals that are not related to stock price can be adjusted for subsequent forfeitures. As noted above, however, options that vest solely based on stock price result in an irreversible expense even if the goal is never met. The option-pricing model used in that situation already would have taken into account the likelihood of the awards never vesting.

Section 423 ESPPs

Tax-qualified ESPPs that are designed to be as generous as the tax code allows now result in an accounting expense, which was not the case under the previous accounting guidance. Now, a plan that offers a discount that is not available to all shareholders and that is greater than the cost of raising capital in a public offering or a plan that has "option-like features"—most notably a look-back feature in which the purchase price is based on the lower of the stock's fair market value on the first or last day of the offering period—must be accounted for under FAS 123(R). The accounting standard contains a safe harbor for discounts of 5% or less.

Bear in mind, however, that the accounting rule does nothing to change Section 423 of the Internal Revenue Code. Companies are still free to design Section 423 ESPPs that offer both a 15% discount and a look-back feature, and participants in such plans are still eligible for preferential tax treatment. This is solely an issue of whether an expense for the plan must be reflected on the income statement.

If the company wishes to avoid incurring an expense in its financial statements for its ESPP, then employees may be allowed no more than 31 days after the start of the purchase period to enroll in the plan (in addition to the plan satisfying the prescribed discount limits discussed above). If the purchase price is set on the last day of the purchase period, then employees may be allowed to withdraw from the offering and have their money returned to them any time before the purchase date without giving rise to an accounting expense. However, if the purchase price is set earlier and participants are allowed to withdraw before the purchase date, then the plan results in an accounting expense.

The expense for Section 423 ESPPs reflects the enrollment date discount and the value of the look-back. To arrive at a fair value, the company must also estimate the amount that will be contributed to the plan and how many shares will be purchased during the offering period.

Restricted Stock Awards and Restricted Stock Units

Unlike stock options and SARs, the full grant date fair value of restricted stock awards and restricted stock units (RSUs) must be recorded as an expense if the shares are granted at no cost to employees. This means the stock's full market value on the grant date will be reflected as an expense. If the employees are required to pay money for the shares, then the accounting expense is the difference between the stock's market value on the grant date and the amount employees must pay for the shares. At first glance, this may appear to be a disincentive to granting such awards. However, grants of full-value awards result in the delivery of fewer shares (often as little as one-third) than awards such as options or SARs that have value only if the stock price rises after the grant date. After all, the restricted stock recipient is receiving an award that is worth something regardless of whether the stock price goes up or down after the grant date. The accounting expense for restricted stock awards and RSUs may not be that different from the expense recognized for stock options and SARs in the same company even thought they provide the employee with fewer shares. The expense is recorded over the vesting period, or expected vesting period in the case of a performance-based award, and can be adjusted for forfeitures unless the performance condition is related to the company's stock price. In the case of a market-based performance award, an option pricing model must be used to determine when and if the award is likely to vest.

Cash-Settled SARs

SARs that are settled in cash are treated as a liability under FAS 123(R), which means that the fair value cannot be determined with finality until the award is exercised or expires. Instead, the company must either use an option-pricing model to estimate the expense at the end of each reporting period in which the award is outstanding using the company's circumstances at that moment or record the award's current intrinsic value. The company must recognize the difference between the current estimate and the previous period's estimate—either as additional expense or as a reversal of previously recognized expense—in the current period.

Phantom Stock

Phantom stock, too, is subject to liability treatment because it pays out in cash. Thus the full expense is not known until the payout date. The full fair market value of the award must ultimately be treated as an expense.

Tax Accounting

In addition to recognizing an expense for equity compensation awards, companies also recognize the tax benefit they expect to reap from awards that are not tax-qualified. Companies receive a tax deduction for amounts that employees must recognize as ordinary income. For equity compensation awards that are not tax-qualified—meaning for everything except ISOs and Section 423 ESPPs—they must estimate how big the tax deduction related to the award will ultimately be when it is exercised or pays out. The company recognizes this estimated tax deduction over the vesting period.

If, at the time of exercise, the company's actual deduction is bigger than expected, the company records the difference (called a "windfall") on its balance sheet as additional paid-in capital. Any windfall amounts are used as credits to cushion any subsequent shortfalls by forming a "pool"; this pool can never fall below zero.

If the company underestimates the actual tax deduction, it will incur a shortfall for the difference between its estimated and actual deductions. If the company does not have sufficient amounts in the pool to offset the shortfall, then the difference between the estimate and the actual tax deduction is recorded as additional expense on the company's income statement.

Making Decisions About Plans: How Important Are Accounting Issues?

When FASB was debating changing equity compensation accounting standards, there was a great deal of concern among public companies that new rules would force them to make drastic changes to their equity compensation practices. It is not clear whether or how much this has actually happened. Research done before the accounting changes was decisive in finding that the changes would not affect stock prices, even though companies were clearly worried that they would. If they do not affect stock prices (because shareholders focus on actual cash flows, not changes in accounting rules), then companies have no other reason to change their granting practices because of the new accounting rules. After all, the rules do not actually change the companies' real costs. But researchers' ability to assess the impact of the new accounting rules was confounded by the fact that at roughly the same time those rules came into effect, the stock exchanges began to require shareholder approval of stock plans, and growing shareholder concern about excessive dilution caused by oversized awards put more pressure on companies to make changes.

One clear result of the accounting changes has been that companies no longer feel constrained to offer only stock options with time-based vesting as their sole or principal equity vehicle. Instead, companies can make choices about which vehicles and performance criteria best suit their compensation needs. Whether the new rules have also caused companies to decrease the total number of awards of any kind they issue is unclear. Equity awards have declined compared to the peak years of the dot-com boom, but that could be for any of the reasons listed above or simply be the result of more normal economic times. Regardless of what has caused what, however, most experts on this topic agree that companies should not let accounting considerations drive their equity practices. In fact FAS 123(R) specifically was intended to neutralize the perceived advantage of stock options so that companies could make appropriate use of the array of stock-based vehicles for compensating their employees.

For closely held companies, the concern about accounting has been much more muted. While companies planning an IPO or a sale want to make their income statements look robust, investors in either case are going to be sophisticated enough to look past accounting norms to assess the real economic state of the company. For companies not planning any of these events soon, the accounting issues are more a matter of making sure that they comply with standards so that their statements will comply with generally accepted accounting principles (GAAP).

CHAPTER 8

Securities Law Considerations

COREY ROSEN AND DANIEL N. JANICH

Closely held companies that compensate employees with equity, either directly or through qualified or nonqualified benefit plans, must be mindful of the complex federal and state securities law considerations that arise as a result. The federal securities laws are primarily the Securities Act of 1933 (the Securities Act) and the Securities Exchange Act of 1934 (the Exchange Act). State securities laws, known as "blue-sky laws," apply to intrastate issuances of securities, not to the more common interstate dealings that trigger application of federal securities laws.

The securities laws are complex, highly technical rules, which, when violated, result in severe penalties. The following discussion merely highlights several of the most significant of these rules. Any securities-related action—including issuing equity compensation to employees—requires a thorough examination and understanding of the securities laws involved.

We begin with a brief review of the registration requirements under the Securities Act, their application to benefit plans, and the most commonly used registration exemptions. What follows is a brief discussion of the Exchange Act's registration and reporting requirements, the anti-fraud rules, and the role played by state securities laws. Finally, because a significant number of closely held companies each year consider public offerings of their shares, we take a brief look at "cheap stock" as a securities-law-related issue that applies to private companies that go public.

Reporting and Disclosure Requirements Under the Federal Securities Laws

The Securities Act and the Exchange Act regulate the offer, purchase, and sale of securities. In several instances, the acts impose reporting and disclosure requirements on employee benefit plans and other related parties.

The Securities Act

The Registration Requirement

The Securities Act provides that securities may not be offered or sold unless a registration statement is filed with the Securities and Exchange Commission (SEC) or an exemption from registration applies. For purposes of the Securities Act, a "sale" of a security is defined as a disposition of the security for "value," i.e., property, cash, or services. To determine whether a plan interest or asset that is being offered or sold by the plan must be registered, the issuer must consider:

- Whether the interest or asset is a security;
- If so, whether the transaction constitutes an offer or sale;
- If so, whether an applicable exemption from registration is available.

Either the participants' individual interests in the employee benefit plan (participation interests) or the assets held by the plan, such as employer stock, may constitute "securities" subject to registration. Thus, for example, an equity compensation vehicle can be issued only if the stock is registered or pursuant to an exemption from registration.

What does registration entail? The registration process requires the issuer to file a registration statement with the SEC before the offer or sale of the securities, and to deliver a prospectus to potential purchasers that provides them with sufficient information to make an informed investment decision. Public companies must register shares and disclose company information as a matter of course.

But private companies with equity compensation plans must either register the shares or offer them subject to an exemption from registration. Private companies must also bear in mind that if they have more than 500 shareholders—which currently includes option holders—they will become de facto public companies subject to the reporting and disclosure requirements of the Securities Act. (As of mid-2007, the Securities and Exchange Commission was considering a change that would exclude the holders of stock options from this number.)

Qualified Retirement and Stock Bonus Plans: Participation Interests

A plan participant's interest in a tax-qualified retirement plan, such as an ESOP, stock bonus plan, or profit sharing plan, that is funded entirely by employer contributions does not constitute a security because such a plan is not both voluntary and contributory. Consequently, a plan sponsor's offer of such interests to employees is not subject to the securities law registration requirements. However, if an employer allows employees to buy employer stock in voluntary contributory plans (such as a 401(k) plan), the SEC generally will consider such interests to be securities. Although the courts have found the securities laws apply only where the plans are both voluntary and contributory, the SEC has taken the position that only voluntary and contributory plans that offer employer stock as an investment option must take the specific step of registering their shares. However, if employer stock is offered by a 401(k) plan solely as a matching contribution made by the employer, those shares will be exempt from registration.

The SEC has found that participation interests in noncontributory ESOPs and stock bonus plans generally do not require registration insofar as no sale is involved. In some cases, closely held companies want to sell stock to their employees through a 401(k) plan and/or ESOP, or solicit employees to move money already in their 401(k) or profit sharing accounts into an ESOP to buy employer stock. Securities law is unclear as to whether this requires a registration if the various exemptions from securities laws are not met.

Registration Exemptions Under the Securities Act

The following discussion summarizes the registration exemptions available under the Securities Act to qualified and nonqualified plans offering employer stock:

1. Exemption of Small Securities Offerings: Regulation A

Regulation A provides for an exemption that acts like simplified registration. It permits issuers to make public offerings of up to $5 million worth of securities in any 12-month period without registration under the Securities Act. Shareholders may use Regulation A to resell up to $1.5 million of securities in any 12-month period. A company using Regulation A must file an offering statement consisting of a notification to potential buyers, an offering circular disclosing financial issues for the offer, and exhibits with the SEC for review. The offering circular is similar in content to a prospectus, but the financial statements are simpler and do not need to be audited. There are no Exchange Act reporting obligations after the offering unless the company has more than $10 million in total assets and more than 500 shareholders.

All types of companies that do not report under the Exchange Act may use Regulation A, except "blank check" companies, those with unspecified businesses, and investment companies registered or required to be registered under the Investment Company Act of 1940. A principal advantage of a Regulation A offering is that it allows a company to test the waters to determine if there is adequate interest in its securities before it incurs the legal, accounting, and other expenses associated with filing an offering statement with the SEC. Under Regulation A, companies can advertise before filing an offering statement, but they cannot solicit or accept money until the SEC has completed its review of the filed statement and investors have been provided with the prescribed offering materials.

2. Private and Limited Offerings: Regulation D

Regulation D, which includes Rules 504, 505, and 506, provides a number of exemptions for small offerings and private placements.

These are among the exemptions sometimes used for equity compensation plans. In each case, the issuer may not use public solicitation or advertising to market the securities and the purchasers receive "restricted" securities, meaning that they may not sell the securities without registration or pursuant to an applicable exemption.[1] Notwithstanding an exemption, the issuer must provide sufficient information to investors to avoid violating the anti-fraud provisions of the securities laws, which are discussed further below.

- Rule 504 provides an exemption for public offerings by issuers for the offer and sale of up to $1 million of securities in a 12-month period. This exemption may be used if the issuer is not a "blank check" company and is not subject to Exchange Act reporting requirements.

- Rule 505, best-known of the Regulation D exemptions, provides an exemption for offerings to any number of "accredited investors" (defined below) and to as many as 35 non-accredited investors when the offers and sales of securities are not in excess of $5 million in any 12-month period. Stock options are counted toward the dollar limit during the entire time they are exercisable. Non-accredited investors must be provided with disclosure documents that generally are the same as those used in registered offerings.

- Rule 506 is a safe harbor for the private offering exemption. This exemption applies to public offerings made to any number of accredited investors and up to 35 other purchases by sophisticated non-accredited investors, without a limit on the amount of money that may be raised. Non-accredited investors must be provided with disclosure documents that generally are the same as those used in registered offerings.

Although companies using Regulation D exemptions are not required to register their securities, after their first securities sales

---

1. "Restricted securities" that cannot be freely resold are distinct from "restricted stock," which is a form of equity compensation.

they must file Form D, a brief notice that discloses the names and addresses of the company's owners and stock promoters.

3. Accredited Investor Exemption

Offers and sales of securities to accredited investors are exempted from registration when the total offering price is less than $5 million. Like the Regulation D exemptions, this exemption does not permit any form of advertising or public solicitation. An accredited investor is:

- a bank, insurance company, registered investment company, business development company, or small business investment company;
- an employee benefit plan, if a bank, insurance company, or registered investment adviser makes investment decisions, or the plan has total assets in excess of $5 million;
- a charitable organization, corporation, or partnership with assets exceeding $5 million;
- a director, executive officer, or general partner of the company selling the securities;
- a business in which all the equity owners are accredited investors;
- a natural person with a net worth of at least $1 million;
- a natural person with income exceeding $200,000 in each of the two most recent years or joint income with a spouse exceeding $300,000 for those years and a reasonable expectation of the same income level in the current year; or
- a trust with assets of at least $5 million, not formed to acquire the securities offered, and whose purchases are directed by a sophisticated person.

4. Exemption for Sales of Securities Through Employee Benefit Plans: Rule 701

Rule 701 was adopted by the SEC to allow privately held companies to offer and sell securities without registration if they are issued to employees as compensation pursuant to written compensatory benefit plans and written compensation contracts. This exemption is often used for equity compensation plan offerings. Issuers may use Rule 701 if they are not subject to the reporting requirements of the Exchange Act, and are not investment companies that must be registered under the 1940 Investment Act.

The aggregate sales price or the amount of securities sold in reliance on Rule 701 during any consecutive 12-month period must not exceed the greater of: (1) $1 million; (2) 15% of the total assets of the issuer (or issuer's parent in cases where the issuer is a wholly owned subsidiary and the securities represent obligations that the parent fully and unconditionally guarantees), as determined on the issuer's most recent balance sheet date; or (3) 15% of the outstanding amount of securities of that class, as determined on the issuer's most recent balance sheet date.

An issuer may sell at least $1 million of securities under this exemption, no matter how small it is. If more than $5 million in securities are expected to be sold in a 12-month period, financial information and risk factors together with a copy of plan-related documents must be disclosed to employees prior to sale in order to satisfy Regulation A disclosure requirements. If such disclosure has not been provided to all investors before the sale, the issuer will lose this exemption.

Volume limitations. The volume limitations of Rule 701 are based solely on actual sales or, as in the case of options, the amounts to be sold. For equity incentives such as restricted stock and compensatory stock purchases, the calculations are made as of the transaction date. For deferred compensation and similar plans, the determination is based upon the date of an irrevocable election to defer compensation. For options, the calculation is made as of the grant date without regard to whether the option is currently exercisable or vested. For securities exchanged solely for consultant and employee services, the value of services is measured by reference to the value of the securities issued rather than to the employee's salary or the consultant's invoice.

5. Exemption of Intrastate Offerings

One well-known exemption applies to securities that are sold entirely within a single state or territory (intrastate offerings). To qualify for this exemption, an issuing company must be incorporated in the state where it is offering the securities, carry out a significant amount of business in that state, and make offers and sales of securities only to residents of that state. To do substantial business in the state, a company must have at least 80% of its gross from the state, at least 80% of its assets located in the state, its principal office located within the state, and at least 80% of the proceeds of the offering used in the state. There is no fixed limit on the size of the offering or the number of purchasers. Practically speaking, however, only very localized businesses can rely on this exemption. Also, it must be remembered that intrastate offerings may be subject to registration requirements under state blue-sky laws.

Form S-8: What If an Exemption from Registration Is Unavailable?

The SEC requires only voluntary contributory employee benefit plans that offer employer stock as an investment option to be registered under the Securities Act. Registration of shares in such plans is intended to afford plan participants a degree of protection insofar as the employer maintains a direct financial interest in soliciting employee contributions to the plan. Form S-8 is a much-simplified federal registration statement available to issuers that are subject to the reporting requirements of the Exchange Act. It may be used only in connection with a compensatory transaction from an employee benefit plan that covers employees of the employer maintaining the plan and/or the employees of its parent and subsidiary corporations.

Form S-8 consists of a prospectus and a registration statement. The prospectus may incorporate a summary plan description, provided the document is dated and clearly identified as constituting part of the prospectus. Other documents may be incorporated by reference in a Form S-8 registration, including the employer's filings made under the Exchange Act with respect to employer securities. Securities registered in this manner are not "restricted securities" for purposes of resale by plan participants other than affiliates.

Registrants that are ineligible to use Form S-8 must use Form S-1. However, extensive disclosure requirements, preparation costs, and annual updating requirements often render use of this form an impractical alternative.

Penalties for Registration Noncompliance

The penalties for failure to comply with the Securities Act registration requirements where an exemption is not available can be severe. A failure to register a security that is not otherwise subject to exemption entitles the purchasers to rescind the transaction and obtain a refund of their purchase price or receive damages. Also, if a registration statement contains a material misstatement or omission, the issuer is automatically liable.

Restricted Securities and the Registration Requirement Upon Resale

A distribution of a security held by the plan to a participant or beneficiary generally does not require registration. Once distributed by the plan, however, the securities may be "restricted," i.e., subject to registration upon resale. Restricted securities generally describe shares issued by a company before its initial public offering (IPO).

Until 90 days after a company's IPO, resales of restricted securities are limited to persons who are not or have not been affiliates of the company for at least three months before the sale. In such case, the seller must have held the restricted securities for at least two years. There is one important exception: 90 days after the shares become subject to the reporting requirements of the Exchange Act, if the stock was granted under Rule 701, option shares issued to non-affiliates can be sold without regard to Rule 144 (except for the manner-of-sale provisions), and affiliates can sell their shares pursuant to Rule 144 (see below), but without regard to the prior holding period.[2] So as not to adversely affect the value of recently issued public shares, it is quite common for companies that issue equity grants in connection with their IPOs to "lock up" or restrict key employees (generally, "affiliates") from selling their shares well beyond the 90-day period imposed under Rule 144, which is described below. A related issue concerns the value of securities that are issued before an IPO. The existence of "cheap stock" is briefly addressed below.

Rule 144 Safe Harbor Exemption for Resale of Securities

Rule 144 of the Securities Act provides a safe harbor exemption from registration for people who want to resell unregistered shares, including those acquired through an equity compensation plan. Rule 144 applies both to sales of "restricted securities" by any person, including plan participants and beneficiaries (unless an applicable registration exemption applies), and to sales of any securities, whether restricted or unrestricted, by affiliates. Rule 144 defines an affiliate as "a person that directly, or indirectly, through one or more intermediaries, controls, or is controlled by, or is under common control with, such issuer."

To obtain the benefit of the exemption, the securities holder must comply with each of Rule 144's five basic requirements:

- *Holding period:* A one-year holding period from the date of acquisition is required for restricted securities. (This may be disregarded if an SEC exemption applies.)
- *Publicly available information:* Required information about the company must be publicly available for at least 90 days before resales.
- *Stock sales:* The stock must be sold through brokers or directly to a market-maker (such as an investment banker).

---

2. As we went to press in mid-2007, the SEC was considering several changes to Rule 144, including the holding periods.

- *Filing requirements:* A Form 144 must be filed with the SEC at the time of any sale, with an exception for sales of fewer than 500 shares for less than $10,000.

- *Volume limitation:* The amount of securities sold in any three-month period may not exceed the greater of: (1) 1% of the outstanding securities; or (2) the average weekly reported volume of trading in these securities for the four calendar weeks preceding the week of the sale.

The SEC has permitted non-affiliate participants to resell securities without registration or exemption from registration where the securities are actively traded, the number of securities involved is relatively small (normally less than 1% of outstanding shares), and the issuer is a reporting entity under the Exchange Act.

The Exchange Act

The Registration Requirement

The Exchange Act mandates that certain issuers comply with additional registration and reporting requirements and trading restrictions. Pursuant to Section 12(g) of the Exchange Act, if an issuer has a class of equity securities held of record by 500 or more persons and the issuer has total assets exceeding $10 million as of the last day of the issuer's fiscal year, the equity securities must be registered under the Exchange Act. Employers that sponsor stock plans will be required to register employer stock and satisfy all reporting requirements of the Exchange Act if Section 12(g)'s criteria apply.

Section 12h-1: Registration Exemption for Employee Benefit Plans

Employee benefit plans themselves are generally exempt from the Exchange Act's registration requirements under Section 12h-1, which exempts participation interests in employee stock bonus, stock purchase, pension, profit-sharing, retirement and other employee benefit plans in which assets are not transferable by the holder (except in the event of death or mental incompetence).

Periodic Reporting

Issuers that have registered their securities under the Securities Act must comply with various periodic and specialized reporting requirements under the Exchange Act as summarized below, but they are not required to formally register under the Exchange Act.

- *Annual reports:* An annual report must be filed on Form 10-K (the form used by most reporting companies), or on Form 11-K (a special annual report for employee stock purchase, savings, and similar plans), as applicable. If a plan registers its participation interests under the Securities Act, the plan will generally be required to file annual reports on Form 11-K. In some circumstances, separate annual reports are not required if the plan combines its Form 11-K with the employer's Form 10-K.

- *Quarterly reports:* Unaudited financial statements and certain additional information must generally be provided within 40 days after the end of each of the first three fiscal quarters for accelerated and large accelerated filers, and 45 days for all other filers. This filing is made on Form 10-Q.

- *Executive compensation disclosures:* Executive compensation disclosure rules apply to proxy statements, periodic reports, and other filings under the Exchange Act, and to registration statements under the Securities Act. The current rules generally require tables disclosing executive pay that furnish details on various types of compensation. The issuer is required to include tables with information on its equity compensation plans.

In 2006, the SEC finalized executive compensation disclosure rules that require disclosure of more details in order to satisfy the registration and reporting requirements. For instance, the rules improve the previous tabular requirements and supplement them with a narrative disclosure section that discusses the material factors underlying compensation policies and decisions reflected in the data presented in tabular form. More detailed disclosures are included in: (1) a Summary Compensation Table that covers compensation, including equity awards, granted during the last fiscal year and two preceding ones; (2) Outstanding Equity Awards at Fiscal Year-End Table and the Options Exercises and Stock Vested tables, which show holdings of equity-related interests that relate to compensation or are potential sources of future gains; and (3) a Retirement Plan and Post-Employment Disclosure Table, which discloses retirement and other post-employment benefits. The reporting requirements are discussed further in the chapter on public company issues.

Specialized Reporting

- *Ad hoc reports:* Form 8-K must be filed whenever events of material importance to security holders, including events relating to executive officer compensation, have occurred. Because of the new executive compensation disclosure rules, the number of Form 8-Ks to be filed each year relating to executive and director compensation matters will likely be reduced.

- *Acquisition reports:* Where a plan acquires beneficial ownership of more than 5% of a class of an issuer's securities registered under the Exchange Act, it must report that ownership by filing a Schedule 13G or Schedule 13D. These filings contain background information about the beneficial owners as well as their investment intentions.

- *Insider reports:* Certain corporate insiders are required under the Exchange Act to report their transactions involving the company's equity securities to the SEC. The reports include information relating to their securities holdings (that are held either inside or outside a plan in which the insider participates), and provide a means for the company to identify and recover profits an insider realizes from the purchase and sale of a company security within a six-month period ("short swing" profits). For this purpose, insiders include every officer, director, and beneficial owner of more than 10% of a company's stock (whether of the sponsoring employer of another company). Many routine plan transactions are exempt from reporting, with the exception of volitional dispositions of employer equity securities and intra-plan transfers of employer equity securities.

Anti-Fraud Rules

Specific state and federal securities rules require disclosure of various categories of information, including objective discussions of risks, the financial condition of the firm, officers' and directors' salaries, as well as other information an employee would need to know to make an informed choice. All securities transactions, including exempt transactions, are subject to the anti-fraud provisions.

The anti-fraud rules of the Securities Act and the Exchange Act prohibit the use of fraud, any manipulative practice, or material misstatement or omission in connection with the offer and sale of securities, whether oral or written. This prohibition of fraud applies to all securities, regardless of whether they have been registered, including plan participation interests that are securities and employer stock held in an employee benefit plan. To ensure compliance with the anti-fraud rules, all "material aspects" of the transaction must be accurately disclosed. These rules apply to employee benefit plans and to plan participants even though the securities that are involved may themselves be exempt from registration.

Proxy Voting and the Sarbanes-Oxley Act of 2002: Plans as Investors

A company with securities registered under the Exchange Act must comply with the SEC proxy rules whenever a shareholder vote is required on corporate matters, including when a publicly held company institutes a new equity compensation plan or modifies an existing plan. The proxy rules require that the company provide a proxy statement to its shareholders, together with a proxy card when soliciting proxies. Proxy statements address management and executive compensation as well as matters that require shareholder votes. If the company is not soliciting proxies but will take a vote on a matter, the company must provide to its shareholders an information statement similar to a proxy statement.

As investors in company stock as well as in other types of securities, qualified employee benefit plans such as ESOPs and 401(k) plans will receive and act upon proxy statements. The securities laws that affect plans in their role as investors3 deal with corporate issues whose discussion, though important, is beyond the scope of this chapter.

State Blue-Sky Laws

The federal and state governments each have their own securities laws and regulations. An issuer must comply with both sets of laws. A particular securities offering that is exempt from registration under the federal securities laws will not necessarily likewise be exempt from registration under state securities laws. Each state has its own securities laws and applicable exemptions. Thus, offerings that are exempt from the provisions of the federal securities laws may still be subject to the notice and filing requirements of various state securities laws.[4] The application of state securities laws to equity compensation plans is discussed in more detail in the NCEO's book *Selected Issues in Equity Compensation.*[5]

Thirty-nine states have blue-sky laws that comply with the Uniform Securities Act, which is partly based on federal law. While some states track federal exemptions; others do not. Explaining each state's rules is beyond the scope of this work, but there are some general patterns:

- States with exemptions similar to Rule 701 are the exception rather than the rule. Those such as California that have such exemptions generally have some additional requirements. State registration of offerings may be needed if the limited-offering exemptions do not apply.

---

3. These issues, which are numerous, include proxy voting by fiduciaries managing plan assets, proxy solicitations by pension funds, the Sarbanes-Oxley provisions prohibiting certain types of executive compensation, and requiring forfeiture of executive compensation in certain circumstances.

4. This does not mean a company has to comply with every state's laws. Rather, they apply in those states in which the employer is actually making an offering.

5. Scott Rodrick, ed. (Oakland, CA: NCEO, 2007), updated annually.

- Most states have limited-offering exemptions for sales to up to 35 non-accredited investors and an unlimited number of accredited investors. Unless the non-accredited investors are deemed to be sophisticated, issuers offering such securities must believe the offering is suitable for these purchasers in terms of their overall financial conditions, which include other securities holdings.

The North American Securities Administrators Association (NASAA), in conjunction with the American Bar Association, has developed the Small Company Offering Registration (SCOR), a simplified "question and answer" registration form that companies also can use as the disclosure document for investors. SCOR was primarily designed for state registration of small-business securities offerings conducted under SEC Rule 504 for sales of securities up to $1 million. Currently, more than 45 states recognize SCOR. To assist small business issuers in completing the SCOR Form, NASAA has developed a detailed "Issuer's Manual" that is available through NASAA's Web site at www.nasaa.org.

In addition, a small company can use the SCOR Form, called Form U-7, to satisfy many of the filing requirements of the SEC's Regulation A exemption for sales of securities of up to $5 million, since the company may file it with the SEC as part of the Regulation A offering statement.

To assist small businesses whose offerings include several states, many states coordinate SCOR or Regulation A filings through a program called regional review. Regional reviews are available in the New England, Mid-Atlantic, Midwest, and Western regions.

Cheap Stock in Pre-IPO Companies

Closely held companies that intend to go public should assess early in their planning stages what their potential securities law issues might be in an IPO. Perhaps the most common securities law concern in pre-IPO companies relates to the existence of what the SEC refers to as "cheap stock."

Companies that go public normally sell their shares at a premium in an IPO when compared to the price at which employee equity awards were granted or stock was sold to employees before the IPO. The reason for this is that once public, the company's stock has a ready market, making it more liquid and thus more valuable. The new equity raised through the IPO also adds value to the company's shares.

Any company contemplating an IPO must consider its ability to attract and retain key talent through this critical period of development. The promise of large monetary gains from stock compensation cashed out after an IPO often substitutes for a significant portion of current salary that would otherwise be required to attract and retain the right set of employees. The temptation for a company to discount the pre-IPO value of its shares in an effort to maximize post-IPO gains may be great under such factual circumstances.

When Does "Cheap Stock" Likely Exist?

If the company discounts its shares too much before the IPO, when compared to the IPO offering price, the SEC, when reviewing the company's IPO registration statement, may treat the pre-IPO issuance as "cheap stock" and require the company to restate its financials, which in turn may delay the effective date of the IPO and adversely affect the IPO stock price. For example, if an IPO is priced at $12, and the company issued awards a year before the IPO at $2, the SEC may audit the financials and find that the true fair market value of the shares was some other number, say $7. It then will require that this additional $5 per share value be included in the financial statement and treated as a compensation cost.

If the earnings per share are reduced as a result of the restatement of financials, this recalculation may result in a reduced IPO share price and consequent loss of equity funds for the company. The company may also be required by the SEC to incur the additional expense of recirculating its prospectus because the financial statements in the initial prospectus were unacceptable.

Companies that are planning IPOs should recognize that the SEC will scrutinize plans issuing stock to employees shortly before the IPO at prices substantially below the IPO price. A company that anticipates cheap stock problems may want to avoid unnecessary delay of its IPO by first consulting with the Office of the Chief

Accountant in the Division of Corporate Finance at the SEC for advice. The company may also want to consider retaining an investment banker to provide an independent appraisal of the fair market value of the company's stock at the grant date. At the very least, a company planning an IPO must be mindful of the factors described in the section on valuation in the introductory chapter of this book, along with the regulations for valuation of stock for deferred compensation purposes, if it desires to avoid the potential problems associated with the existence of cheap stock.

CHAPTER 9

Special Considerations for Public Companies

COREY ROSEN

Most of this book deals with issues and ideas that apply to both public and private companies. Publicly traded companies, however, have a variety of specific concerns that either do not apply to closely held companies or are less significant for them.

Reporting Requirements for Executive Compensation

Publicly traded companies have a variety of disclosure requirements related to equity compensation for executives. Rules created in 2006 require disclosure of the last three fiscal years of compensation for the chief executive officer and the three other most highly compensated executives based on total compensation, excluding any increases in pension values and nonqualified deferred compensation. Anyone who served as chief executive or financial officer in the most recent fiscal year covered by the disclosures must also be included, even if they are no longer serving in the role. Small-business issuers[1] have to report only on the compensation of the CEO and the two other top-paid executives for the past two fiscal years, and do not have

---

1. A small business issuer is an issuer with less than $25 million in revenues in its last fiscal year and with outstanding publicly held stock worth less than $25 million.

as many disclosure requirements. Several specific reports must be filed for equity awards to covered individuals.

Executive compensation tables: In the Summary Compensation Table, companies must disclose (among other compensation elements) all stock awards, based on grant date fair value as determined under accounting standard FAS 123(R).[2] This includes options, bonus shares, performance shares, restricted stock, phantom stock, stock appreciation rights (SARs), and restricted stock units (RSUs). Additionally, any increases in pension values, nonqualified deferred compensation, and earnings on any equity awards (such as dividends on restricted stock) must also be disclosed. Employer contributions to qualified defined contribution plans must be included. Qualified employee stock purchase plans (ESPPs), although technically a kind of option, are not included. The table is denominated in dollars, not in the number of shares or some other measure. A separate appendix summarizes grants of plan-based awards. These are not the same as the equity compensation tables discussed below. They also must be discussed in a plain-English narrative. (A similar table is required for director compensation.)

Equity compensation tables: Equity compensation must be described in a number of tables. Companies must disclose: (1) the number of securities to be issued upon exercise of outstanding options, warrants, and rights; (2) key terms of outstanding options, warrants, and rights; and (3) the number of securities remaining for further issuance, excluding those in item 1.

This is in addition to disclosures required under FAS 123(R), which include options outstanding at the beginning of the year, end of the year, and during the year; options exercised and/or forfeited during those times; terms of significant modifications; the range of exercise prices; the weighted-average exercise price of equity awards; and the weighted average remaining contractual exercise price of the awards. These requirements are for all awards, not just those to executives.

The proxy disclosure rules require several additional tables, including those covering performance-based awards granted to ex-

---

2.   For more information on this standard, see the accounting chapter of this book.

ecutives as well as all other equity plans. Generally, companies must indicate the number of awards issued, the grant date fair value of the awards, the exercise prices, unexercised awards, the expiration dates, and other details. An additional table provides information on outstanding awards at the end of the year, while one more table looks at director awards. A discussion of granting practices must be included as well, specifically discussing whether any awards can be modified (backdated, repriced, etc.), how awards are issued, how grant timing is determined, and other granting practices. If the exercise price is not the stock's closing price on the grant date, the company must explain why that is the case.

Requirements for Executive Equity Trading

Section 16 of the Securities Act of 1934 and the Sarbanes-Oxley Act of 2002 impose a significant number of requirements on securities holdings, purchases, and sales by officers, directors, and more-than-10% owners of public companies. These "reporting persons" or "insiders" include executives who are named officers and those considered to have significant policy-making authority in the company. Laws and regulations covering these issues are long and complex and described only generally here.[3]

Under Section 16(a) of the 1934 Act, as amended by the Sarbanes-Oxley Act, these insiders must comply with a variety of securities reporting requirements. They must report their holdings in company stock within 10 days of becoming subject to Section 16. And they must report sales and purchases of stock, grants or exercises of options, amendments of options, grants of equity in other forms, and similar transactions within two business days of the transaction date. For their part, employers are required to report any delinquencies in these filings in their proxy statements.

Under Section 16(b) of the 1934 Act, companies must recover any "profits" made by reporting persons who buy and sell company

---

3. For a more detailed description of federal securities laws, please see William R. Pomierski and William J. Quinlan, Jr., "Federal Securities Law Considerations for Equity Compensation Plans" in *Selected Issues in Equity Compensation* (Oakland, CA: NCEO, updated annually).

stock within six months. These "short-swing profits" do not necessarily match the insider's actual profits. Instead, to arrive at the amount the insider owes the company, the company matches the highest sale price against the lowest purchase price, the second-highest sale price against the second-lowest purchase price, and so on within a six-month period. The transactions that are matched do not have to involve the same shares; the law simply looks to the number bought and sold out of total holdings. This recovery is not limited to cases where the insider is in possession of insider information.

Some transactions between the company and the executive are exempt from these rules, including most grants of options and other equity awards, provided they are awarded in compliance with specific corporate governance procedures, e.g., the specific grant is approved by the board, a committee of non-employee directors, or shareholders, or they may not be exercised for at least six months after issuance.[4]

Once the shares are held, they are subject to the six-month rule, but again certain transactions are exempt from Section 16(b) if they are approved in advance by the board, a board committee, or shareholders. These include dispositions back to the issuer for a variety of reasons, most notably to pay the exercise price of an option, the cash settlement of a SAR, and the surrender of an option or SAR in connection with the grant of a replacement award. Transactions that are the result of a merger may also qualify for exemption from Section 16(b).

Insiders must also refrain from trading in company securities when they are in possession of "material nonpublic information." Insiders can exercise options or SARs while in possession of such information, but they can't sell the shares under those conditions. The most common way to avoid this is to institute a "Section 10b5-1" trading plan, a binding written contract under which shares are bought or sold pursuant to a predetermined schedule.

---

4.   For a more detailed description of Rule 16b exemptions, see William R. Pomierski and William J. Quinlan, Jr., "Federal Securities Law Considerations for Equity Compensation Plans" in *Selected Issues in Equity Compensation* (Oakland, CA: NCEO, updated annually).

A company may rely on Rule 701, which provides an exemption from securities registration for offers of securities to employees, directors, officers, consultants and advisors, and certain family members, allowing them to sell shares 90 days after the company's initial public offering. Affiliates (all directors and certain executive officers) are subject to the additional restrictions and selling requirements of Rule 144. These restrictions are in addition to whatever requirements investment banks may impose on employees selling their shares after an IPO.

Dilution Issues

Although much recent discussion about changes in equity compensation plans has revolved around the impact of the new accounting rules, concerns about shareholder dilution probably have been more central in determining corporate behavior. Shareholder approval rules implemented in 2003 and described below made it more difficult to obtain approval for equity plans just as shareholder ire was rising about excesses in stock option grants, especially for executives.

In the late 1990s, it was not unusual for companies to have overhang rates from options of 15% or more, especially in the technology sector. ("Overhang" is the number of unvested options outstanding plus the number of shares authorized to be issued for options not yet awarded, divided by the total number of outstanding shares.) Investors were comfortable with that when stock prices continued to go up but became more concerned when prices headed the other way. Institutional investor advisory group Institutional Shareholder Services, for example, in 2006 amended its guidelines for overhang and "burn rates" (the number of shares or options awarded each year as a percentage of outstanding shares) to recommend voting against any company whose three-year average burn rate for equity awards exceeds one standard deviation from its industry norm and is higher than 2% of common shares outstanding. A company can still get a yes vote if it commits to reducing its burn rate to the industry mean. At the time that policy was amended, the mean in larger public companies ranged from 0.94% to 5.02% and in smaller public companies from 2.03% to 6.92%.

Companies have responded to this in various ways. The most common approach is to issue restricted stock. It takes many more options to provide the same economic value as restricted stock, because restricted stock has value for the recipient even if the share price goes down. The smaller grant sizes mean less shareholder dilution, although they do not decrease economic dilution if the restricted stock is designed to have the same economic value. Stock-settled SARs are also less dilutive in terms of shares, but, again, are by definition as dilutive economically if they are designed to provide the same value to participants as options. In either case, companies can lower share dilution by using more cash per award or use less cash but issue more awards. It's a bigger piece of a smaller pie versus a smaller piece of a bigger pie.

Stock Exchange Shareholder Approval Rules[5]

Since 2003, companies listed on the New York Stock Exchange (NYSE) and the NASDAQ have been required to obtain shareholder approval for all equity compensation plans, with certain very narrow exceptions.

The two sets of rules are very similar. Below are the key requirements.

1. *Scope:* All equity compensation plans and any material revisions to these plans must be approved by shareholders, with certain narrow exceptions outlined below.

2. *Equity compensation plans defined:* An equity compensation plan includes any plan or other arrangement to deliver securities to employees, including options. The term does not include dividend reinvestment plans or plans that allow employees, directors, or other service providers to buy shares on the open market for current fair market value.

---

5. This material is adapted from Alisa J. Baker, *The Stock Options Book, 8th ed.* (Oakland, CA: NCEO, 2007).

3. *Material modification:* "Material" is not defined by these rules, although it specifically does not include the limitation of rights and benefits associated with a plan; only modifications expanding employee rights and benefits are covered. The list of covered modifications includes:

   a. A material increase in the number of shares available, other than for stock splits, corporate reorganizations, and similar arrangements. Evergreen plans require approval for each increase unless the plan has a term of not more than 10 years. If the increase is not pursuant to a formula, then shareholders must approve each increase. A requirement that grants be made out of treasury or repurchased shares will not, in itself, be considered a formula.

   b. An expansion of the types of awards available under the plan or of the class of employees, directors, or other service providers eligible to participate.

   c. A material extension of the term of the plan.

   d. A material change in the method of determining the strike price of options, such as changing the fair market value from the closing price on the grant date to the average of the high and low price on the grant date.

   e. The deletion or limitation of any provision prohibiting repricing.

4. *Repricings:* Unless a plan specifically permits repricing, it is considered to prohibit it. Any actual repricing is thus considered a material modification. Canceling an option and substituting a new award pursuant to a merger, acquisition, spin-off, or similar transaction is not included.

5. *Employment inducement awards:* If the company's independent compensation committee approves them, inducement awards to new hires may be made without shareholder approval. Companies must disclose in a press release, and in written material for the NYSE, a description of the award, its terms, the number of shares and its recipient. "New hires" includes rehires of previ-

ous employees following a "bona fide" period of non-employment.

6. *Mergers and acquisitions:* Shareholder approval is not required to replace options or other awards in a transaction. Shares available for award at a closely held company that is acquired may be used in post-acquisition grants, provided that the plan existed before the merger or acquisition being contemplated. The time the shares are available cannot be extended after the transaction.

7. *Qualified plans:* Employee stock ownership plans, other Section 401 plans invested in company stock (401(k), profit sharing, and stock bonus plans), and Section 423 employee stock purchase plans do not require approval.[6]

8. *Parallel excess plans:* These are plans that provide additional company contributions or employee deferrals into qualified plans that limit the total amount of compensation that can be considered or place ceilings on the total amounts that can be contributed. Companies sometimes make up the difference that would be allowed if these ceilings did not exist; the contributions or deferrals are not tax-favored. Investments in equity in these plans would be exempted from shareholder approval requirements. The plan must cover all or substantially all affected employees, its terms must be the same for those covered, it must parallel the terms for the qualified plans, and no one can receive compensation in excess of 25% of cash compensation.

9. *Broker voting:* Broker-held shares ("street name" shares) cannot be voted by proxy by the brokers unless the beneficial owner provides specific instructions.

Governance Requirements

NYSE and NASDAQ rules require independent compensation committees to approve the compensation of CEOs and other executives,

---

6. Note, however, that the tax rules contained in Section 423 of the Internal Revenue Code do require shareholder approval of Section 423 employee stock purchase plans.

including equity awards. While not required, it is good practice for compensation consultants to be hired by and report to the board only.

Fiduciary Concerns for Qualified Plans

For public companies, the role of employer stock in qualified plans such as ESOPs and 401(k) plans has declined markedly since debacles at Enron and other companies at which employee retirement funds were excessively invested in company stock. In 401(k) plans, for instance, the percentage of overall investments in company stock declined to 11% in 2007 from 19% just five years earlier. Most of the problems came in 401(k) plans that offered company stock as an investment choice, and often had company matching contributions invested in company stock as well. Some public companies used the ESOP contribution to constitute the 401(k) match. Stand-alone ESOPs, by contrast, have had fewer problems, largely because they generally run side-by-side with diversified plans. The employee risk in these plans is lower because they have a diversified account to fall back on if the ESOP falters.

More than 60 lawsuits were filed in response to the rapid decline in stock value in companies where employees were heavily invested in employer stock. Those that have settled have provided relatively small amounts for employees, with an average payout of less than $100 per participant, and rarely more than a few hundred dollars. Some settlements, however, required changes in plan structure. Although the per-participant amounts have been small, the total costs, including legal fees, have often been in the tens of millions of dollars or more. A few of the lawsuits have been dismissed, but about half are still in process.

While the legal issues about who has standing to sue, when a company must disclose adverse financial information, exactly who is a fiduciary, and to what extent plan documents can require fiduciaries to hold on to employer shares are all still largely unresolved, some key trends are emerging:

- Boards have a responsibility to monitor, not just appoint, plan fiduciaries.

- Corporate officers can be deemed to be fiduciaries, even if not named as fiduciaries, if they cause fiduciaries to take actions or make false or misleading claims about company stock.

- Securities laws probably will not provide much protection for fiduciaries who fail to provide material information about impending major problems at the company, even if this means informing participants before the pubic (which would violate securities laws). Companies may have to disclose information publicly to avoid this potential liability.

- Independent fiduciaries can provide some protection if they genuinely can make decisions in what they see as participants' best interests.

- Laws providing that ESOPs (as opposed to 401(k) plans) are designed to invest primarily in company stock provide considerable, but not complete, protection against decisions to hold or purchase stock in the face of stock price pressures. Where fiduciaries know, or should know, that the company is facing problems that could imperil its future, however, they should consider selling company stock in the plan and suspending further acquisitions.

In 2006, Congress passed the Pension Protection Act. Public companies with stock in their 401(k) plans (including KSOPs that combine an ESOP and a 401(k) plan) are now required to allow employees to diversify out of employer stock at any time if the stock was purchased with their own deferrals or after three years of service if purchased with employer contributions. Stand-alone ESOPs in public companies and all closely held company ESOPs are exempted. For stock contributed by the company in a plan year beginning before January 1, 2007, the company may phase in the new diversification rules (except for certain employees) over a three-year transition period at 33% per year.

CEOs and Everyone Else

The public concern (and often outrage) about equity compensation has centered on CEO equity and, to a lesser extent, on other top executives. Yet to the extent companies have responded, they have typically cut non-executive employees' eligibility for equity awards. About one-third of broad-based plans have become substantially less broad-based as a result. While many companies are reducing the number of options going to top executives, they are usually replacing these with some other form of equity or incentive. That is only rarely the case for other employees, however. CEO compensation, in fact, has continued to rise far faster than inflation, median wages, and shareholder returns.

This behavior may be rational for CEOs, but it is hardly rational for companies. As we pointed out earlier in this book, broad-based plans deliver a lot more per dollar invested than narrowly focused plans. The corrosive effect on morale of eliminating or reducing employee awards while maintaining or fattening executive rewards that are already oversized is a much more serious concern than whatever impact broad-based plans may have on financial statements or shareholder relations.

As companies navigate all the changes in equity requirements that have developed over the last few years, it is important to keep in mind that the goal of equity compensation must first be to provide ways to attract, motivate, and reward employees in a way that is beneficial to both them and shareholders. Designing plans either to find clever ways to get executives more without running afoul of these new requirements, or to minimize accounting or dilution charges even at the expense of effective programs is shortsighted and counterproductive for all involved.

CHAPTER 10

Designing an Equity Incentive Plan

COREY ROSEN

A variety of issues must be considered when designing an equity compensation plan for employees. This chapter is not intended to provide specific guidelines on how to structure a plan but rather to raise the issues companies need to consider. In making these decisions, company leaders should consult with peers and advisors as well as evaluate available survey data on industry practices.

How Much to Share

The first decision is how much ownership to share. This issue will differ for closely held companies and public companies, so each kind of company is looked at separately.

Closely Held Companies

The most typical way owners of closely held companies decide how much ownership to share is by setting aside an amount of stock that does not exceed the maximum dilution level with which they are comfortable. (The exception to this is when the plan is an employee stock ownership plan [ESOP], in which case the goal is generally for owners to sell some or all of their stock to the plan.) This approach can create problems, however.

Typically, once this number is set, a large portion of those shares is either provided immediately to existing employees or allocated to employees over a few years. The problem with this strategy is that allocating too much too quickly leaves relatively few shares to give to new employees. In a growing company, that can create a severe problem in attracting and retaining good people. It can also create two classes of employees, some with large equity grants and some without them. Moreover, this model often does not create an explicit link between employee effort and the rewards of ownership.

A second approach focuses on what percentage of compensation must be provided in the form of equity in order to attract, retain, and motivate people. These decisions need to be based on a sense of what people can get elsewhere, as well as on discussions with employees to get a sense of how much they expect.

Rather than thinking about "how much" in terms of a total percentage of company shares or total compensation, it might make sense to use a more dynamic model based on performance. In this approach, the issue for existing owners is not "what percentage of the company do we own," but "how much is what we own worth?" Owners in this model would rather own 10% of a $10 million company than 90% of a $1 million company. This notion can be made into an explicit plan by telling employees that if the company meets or exceeds certain targets, they will get a percentage of the incremental value created by that performance in the form of equity or something equivalent to equity, such as phantom stock. If the company exceeds its goals, then, by definition, sharing part of the surplus value leaves both the employees and the existing owners better off than they would have been. The targets can be anything—sales, profits, market penetration, or whatever else is critical to the company's future.

It is also important, as the chapter on executive compensation describes in more detail, to consider the "internal equity" of awards. A common problem in equity plans is that employees believe they are not getting what they deserve, something they assess primarily based on what they perceive other people to be getting. Few employees would argue that everyone should get the same, but most would contend that everyone should get awards consistent with their relative contributions to the company. This problem has been starkest in relationship to executive pay, but even at rank-and-file levels, it is not uncommon for companies to pay people doing very similar jobs very different amounts of equity, perhaps because of the timing of when they came to work (more awards were available or the shares were more opportunely priced) or what it was perceived to take to hire them. Nobel Prize-winning research has shown that perceived equity in economic transactions will often trump purely "rational" economic logic. Even if you can show that giving top executives outsized grants helps everyone in the company, if employees believe that what they get is not equitable relative to what the top executives get, they will be more cynical and less motivated.

Closely held companies need to beware of the possibility of making equity grants to so many employees that the grants create legal or regulatory problems. An S corporation, for instance, cannot have more than 100 shareholders, and option holders count as shareholders (an ESOP or 401(k) plan counts as only one, however). If any corporation has more than 500 shareholders, it becomes a de facto public company. (As of this writing the SEC has proposed an exception from the 500-shareholder rule for stock options granted to employees or other service providers under a written plan.) Finally, equity plans may be subject to securities laws. This issue is described in more detail in the chapter on securities law considerations, as well as briefly in this chapter.

Publicly Traded Companies

Publicly traded companies face many of the same design issues as their closely held counterparts and may want to use some of the same decision guidelines. Their principal constraint is investor concern about dilution. Dilution is usually measured by "overhang," the number of awards outstanding plus the number of shares available to be issued divided by all of the company's outstanding common shares. "Run rate" is another common measure of dilution; it is the annual percentage of shares outstanding that need to be issued each year to satisfy equity awards. This amount varies by company. In broad-based equity plans, we find that most companies fall in the 5% to 15% range, with very large public companies often in the lower end of the range and technology companies and younger companies in the higher end. Many large investors and investor advisory services have rules of thumb for dilution or run rates from equity grants, usually at dilution under 10% and run rates under 3%.

Simple calculations of overhang and run rates do have an important flaw in estimating the dilutive effect of equity awards, however. One option counts the same as one share of restricted or other full-value stock award. Phantom stock and stock appreciation rights not settled in shares do not count at all. Stock-settled stock appreciation rights (SARs) result in dilution only once the shares are paid out. Thus, a grant of 1,000 stock-settled SARs would likely have a less dilutive effect than the grant of 1,000 stock options because only enough shares to cover the appreciation of the SARs will be issued upon exercise, even though the economic effect for the award recipient is the same with SARs as it is with stock options. One share of restricted stock is typically worth about three options, so restricted stock generates only one-third the measured dilution. Simply focusing on share dilution as measured by overhang and run rates, therefore, can be misleading. The real issue ultimately is overall economic dilution. Institutional Shareholder Services, the largest shareholder advisory service, handles this by weighting the number of full-value awards depending on a company's volatility. A company with very volatile stock must count each full-value award such as restricted stock as 1.5 option shares, while companies with low volatility must weight each full-value award the same as four option shares.

What Kind of Equity?

The kind (or kinds) of equity vehicles a company chooses depends largely on the purposes of the plan. While that may seem obvious, it is far too common for companies to pick an equity vehicle because "that's what other people do," or "that's what my advisor understood best," or "I didn't know there were other ways to do it." Beware too of advisors whose discouragement of one kind of plan or another may really be a way of saying, "I don't know how to do the other types."

ESOPs are the vehicle of choice for closely held companies whose owners want to use ownership sharing for business continuity. These plans also make sense in companies that have a strong commitment to sharing ownership broadly and find the ESOP rules acceptable, given the tax benefits the plans provide. ESOPs do not work for companies that want to discriminate in terms of who gets awards or (in most cases) where the philosophy is that employees should have to buy stock to become owners. Contributing company stock to employees' 401(k) plan accounts makes sense for companies that want to share ownership broadly and are comfortable with the allocation and diversification rules. Companies that want to provide a tax-favored way for employees to invest can make company stock an investment option in their 401(k) plans but can no longer force employees to buy company stock with their own contributions. Generally, ESOPs and 401(k) plans are not means for providing incentives for individual behavior; instead, they provide incentives for employees as a group. Employee stock purchase plans (ESPPs) are a terrific benefit, but only a few companies will have active or substantial enough participation to make them a key element of their ownership cultures on their own. They are also less incentive plans than a way to reward employees.

Very small companies with no plans to be acquired or go public often want to use cash-settled SARs or phantom stock because they can be used to track equity changes but are simple and do not require actual stock to be issued. They lack some of the connotation of ownership, however, and offer no favorable tax treatment. Stock options and restricted stock, in contrast, require that the company provide some form of liquidity for the shares, often through a public offering or sale, although companies can also simply arrange to repurchase the shares.

Unlike stock options and SARs, restricted stock and restricted stock units (RSUs) deliver actual shares to employees even if the stock price declines after they are granted. There are pros and cons to this approach. On the one hand, employees do not end up with nothing just because share prices decline in the market generally. On the other hand, some have argued that restricted stock just provides "pay for pulse," and that it is thus less of an incentive than options or SARs. Restricted stock can cause more economic dilution than options or SARs (because options are exercisable only if the price of the stock goes up), but it causes less shareholder dilution in terms of the number of shares outstanding because grant sizes are smaller. That is because the risk protection of restricted stock means that each share granted is worth more than each option or SAR. A ratio of one restricted stock share to three or four stock options is not uncommon, for instance. Stock-settled SARs also pay out in shares, but are usually less dilutive than stock options, because only the number of shares needed to cover the appreciation in the stock price between grant and exercise must be issued, usually minus whatever amount is need to pay taxes.

Stock option plans can allow for the granting of nonqualified stock options (NSOs), just incentive stock options (ISOs), or some of both. Most broad-based option plans provide NSOs for rank-and-file employees because few of these employees will be able or want to meet the buy-and-hold conditions that make ISOs eligible for favorable tax treatment. Many of those who do hold onto the shares, moreover, will not get a large benefit from being able to pay taxes at capital gains rather than ordinary income rates. Companies reason that, because the employees will not use the benefits of ISOs anyway, they might as well grant NSOs and get a more certain corporate tax deduction.

Many companies do, however, grant ISOs to highly paid employees, who can greatly benefit from capital gains treatment and who may demand such options to come to work for or stay with a company. All-ISO plans are also common in startup companies that are not worried about tax deductions (because there are no profits) and thus are willing to give all employees the possibility of capital gains treatment on their options. ISOs also work well where the share price is low and thus the company is not likely to run up against the $100,000 limit on ISOs becoming exercisable in a year.

One problem with options and any form of SARs is that, as valuation models show, volatility is the single most important factor in determining their value. To understand this, imagine two companies with stock price movements as shown in table 10-1.

Stolid has had steady, if unexciting, performance. Up & Down's performance has been exciting, but the company has done less well

Table 10-1

	Up & Down Inc.	Stolid Corporation
Price at vesting date	$10	$10
Price one year later	$17.75	$11.20
Price two years later	$9.00	$12.00
Price three years later	$14.50	$13.30
Price four years later	$21.00	$15.00
Price five years later	$10.00	$16.20

for long-term investors. If CFO Joe Smith had 1,000 vested options at the start of year one and at least another five years to exercise, he would have done reasonably well, but not great, in any year if he had exercised and sold the stock. If Mary Jones had 1,000 vested options with the same terms as Joe, she would be in a much better situation if she had been astute or lucky enough to exercise and sell the shares in three of the five years. So valuation models say Mary's options are worth more at grant than Joe's even though, long-term, Mary's company is an unimpressive performer. Mary and other top officers are being rewarded for movement in the company's stock, not for long-term growth.

This has a number of insidious effects. First, it can encourage excessive risk-taking by top decision-makers, especially if their expected time horizon with the company is short (as it tends to be these days). Second, it introduces a lottery effect into the incentive structure. If Joe goes to work when the stock is at $7, and Mary joins a little later when it is at $14, Joe has a chance to make a lot of money, but Mary can only make a fraction as much. Finally, it can engender cynicism among employees who view options as a lottery whose benefits may go to the lucky and to the insiders who know best when to exercise.

This does not mean options or SARs are never appropriate. They can make sense for companies with rapidly appreciating share prices or where boards want employees to benefit only from increases in stock value. By issuing options in smaller amounts more often, moreover, much of the lottery effect described here can be ameliorated or avoided.

Who Is Eligible and Who Will Actually Get Equity?

In the past, the answer to the question of who was eligible was very simple for most companies: just the "key" people. In some ways, this is still how companies view equity; it is just that their definition of "key" has changed. For many companies, everyone is a key person. Many companies are pushing down more decision-making to all levels of the company, asking employees to make business decisions on a regular basis. Managers at these companies reason that if they want people to think and act like owners, they should make them owners. At the same time, for some companies in some labor markets, it is necessary to provide options at all levels just to attract and retain people.

For companies in these situations, the answer to "who's eligible?" is simple—everyone is. Other companies choose more complex approaches that take several criteria into account. This discussion is only for plans other than ESOPs, 401(k)s, and Section 423 ESPPs, for which there are specific rules about eligibility.

One set of issues that some companies consider, but that they probably should not, is the so-called "1/n" or "free rider" effect, and the related "line-of-sight" problem. The argument here is that an equity award cannot be much of an incentive to an employee who cannot see (has no line of sight to) just how his or her work actually affects stock prices. This is especially problematic in larger organizations where employees not only don't have clear lines of sight to the awards but also figure they can "free ride" on the efforts of others.

These arguments are appealing but empirically wrong. Research shows that motivation at work is much more complicated than a simple economic calculation. Few employees go to work each day thinking, "If I do x, I get y, but if I do x + a, I get y + b, so if y + b is large enough, I'll do x + a." A good test is to ask yourself whether anyone you know well really thinks this way. Research shows again and again that most people's efforts at work are a function of how well their job functions fit their skills, whether they have opportunities for meaningful input into decisions affecting their jobs, how much they trust management and management trusts them, whether they find the job engaging, and whether they believe what they and the company do has value.

Equity sharing becomes important in this context not so much as an incentive for behavior but as a reward. If people are asked to act like owners and are treated like owners, they will be more productive and make larger contributions in terms of new ideas and information. If they then are denied an opportunity to benefit from what they add, they will feel manipulated and back away. If, on the other hand, they feel they are equitably rewarded relative to what others contribute or that they are all part of a team sharing in the results, they are much more likely to stay committed. So the question of who gets equity should be based on who you want thinking and acting like an owner.

Tenure

At the simplest level, companies can require that people work a minimum amount of time, often one year, before they become eligible for equity. This assures the employee has at least some commitment to the company.

Full-Time/Part-Time

In the past, it was unusual to provide equity to part-time employees. Innovators like Starbucks, however, have provided options to everyone, arguing that many of their part-time people would (or if properly rewarded could) be long-term employees.

Performance or a Universal Rule?

Equity can be granted according to some kind of merit judgment; on a regular, universal schedule such as annually, or upon hiring or promotion; or it can be granted or vest upon the achievement of an individual, group, or corporate objective. These methods are not mutually exclusive; many companies use a combination of these techniques.

The core issue here is that, on the one hand, including every-one who is eligible according to some formula rules out discretion, which employees may see as arbitrary or political. It also may help foster a team atmosphere in which everyone sees that they have a stake. On the other hand, some employees may feel cheated if they think they have been exceptional performers but get unexceptional rewards. That can make some combination appealing, provided the basis for rewarding excellence is one that most or all employees see as reasonably fair—a tricky business, but one many companies have done well at, albeit in a variety of ways. Some companies, for instance, use 360-degree performance reviews in which everyone reviews everyone else, others use very specific and transparent financial or other measurable targets, and others seek employee input in designing rating systems.

A typical merit-based approach would provide work unit manag-ers (or a single manager in a smaller company) with a number of awards that can be granted to employees in the group based on a performance appraisal. An alternative to individual merit judgments is to provide that a pool of equity awards will be given to a work team on the achievement of their own goals. Many companies, of course, will simply name specific individuals, usually top managers, who will get equity, but the company will define how much they get based on some merit assessment.

At the other end of the spectrum is an automatic formula based on compensation, seniority, promotion, or some other work-related, measurable construct. This can be for one employee or every em-ployee. For instance, a number of larger companies provide all em-ployees who meet basic service requirements with 10% of pay every year in stock options. The argument behind such formulas is that compensation reflects management's judgment of an employee's contribution to the company, and equity is simply another form of compensation.

Many companies provide awards on hiring, then make addi-tional grants periodically or upon promotion. Linking additional grants to promotion gives employees an incentive to improve their skills and rewards those people the organization believes are mak-ing greater contributions. On the other hand, an overemphasis on promotion-related grants can mean that employees who are very good performers but who are not in jobs that can easily lead to a promotion are overlooked.

Refresher grants give employees additional awards when they exercise some of the options or other equity benefits they were previously granted. For instance, if an employee has 1,000 options and exercises 200, then the employee would be given new options on another 200 shares at exercise. The theory here is to maintain a constant level of equity interest in the company. Similarly, refresher awards might be granted when the company issues additional shares so that an employee maintains the same percentage of potential ownership as was held before the dilution (this feature is more common for executive plans). While these automatic additional grants help to keep the employee's equity interest high, shareholders might object to the ongoing dilution.

How Often Should Awards Be Granted?

Equity inherently involves risk, but the design of plans can accentuate that risk. Companies that provide one-time grants of stock options or SARs or grant them only upon an event, such as hiring, promotion, or meeting some corporate target, wind up with employees whose ownership interest in the company is based on the price of stock at a single point in time. This is not a problem with full-value awards, which do not have an exercise price based on the stock's trading price on the grant date.

Granting options or SARs infrequently accelerates the risk of equity both for the employee and the company because equity granted at a high price may never be "in the money"; awards granted at a low price may cost the company more than it intended when they are redeemed. Employees who happen to get their chunk of equity at a good time end up doing very well, while those who get their grants when the price is not so favorable don't do well at all. Creating an ownership culture of "we're all in this together" can be very difficult in these circumstances.

For many companies, the best way to deal with these potential problems is to provide grants in smaller amounts but more frequently or to grant full-value awards such as restricted stock or phantom stock. Frequent grants work best for companies using equity as a compensation strategy. Startups whose stock value is close to zero anyway or that use large initial grants to attract people away from other opportunities may find this less appropriate. It also won't work for companies that want simply to make grants at the occasional discretion of the company, often on the attainment of some corporate milestone. These companies see equity more as a symbolic reward than as ongoing ownership strategy.

Smaller but more frequent grants are easiest to do in public companies where the share price is readily ascertainable and where share prices change continually. In a closely held company, there is no point in granting equity more frequently than the stock is valued. Giving an employee a grant three times a year when the price per share is determined annually, for instance, would give the employee three sets of awards all at the same price.

Periodic allocation "dollar-cost averages" the awards, smoothing bumps in volatile markets. This approach also gives employees more of a long-term, ongoing stake in the company. With the vesting schedules attached to the repeated grants of awards, employees are provided an even longer-term interest in the company's performance. Finally, there will be fewer big winners and losers among employees with otherwise similar jobs.

Frequent grants are not all good news, of course. The more often awards are granted, the more complex their administration becomes. Even with the best software, there is much more data entry, many more forms to file and disseminate, and many more errors that can be made.

When Will Employees Be Able to Use the Awards?

There are two principal issues in deciding when employees will be able to translate their equity into cash: vesting and exercise periods. Vesting generally provides that an employee accrues an increasing right to the awards granted based on the number of years worked. However, companies also sometimes use performance vesting, in which vesting is a function of company, group, or individual performance. As various targets are met, the equity awards become increasingly vested. The exercise period is the time between an award's vesting and its expiration.

By far the most common exercise period for stock options is 10 years; there are no data on SARs. Some exercise periods are shorter, but they are rarely longer. There is nothing magical about 10 years for NSOs, but for ISOs, the exercise period cannot exceed 10 years. The more volatile a company's stock, the more important a longer exercise period is so that employees can weather the downturns.

As for vesting, the patterns on time-based vesting are fairly consistent across companies, with three- to five-year graduated vesting the most common schedule. Sales or profit targets are the most common performance triggers. A few companies allow employees to exercise their awards only when a defined event occurs, such as the achievement of a certain stock price or earnings goal. This accomplishes two things. First, it provides an incentive to meet the goal, and second, it reassures investors that dilution will occur only if the company meets certain targets. Once these targets are met, employees are normally given a certain amount of time to exercise the award, anywhere from a few months to several years. Alternatively, a company could provide that awards can be exercised only upon the occurrence of an event, such as a sale or going public.

Deciding whether to provide for immediate vesting upon an IPO or the sale of the company, even if the awards would not otherwise be vested, can be difficult. This clearly provides a good benefit for employees, but it may make it more difficult to sell a company or take one public, especially if buyers perceive that employees will now have fully vested options that, if the underlying stock can also then be sold, may be valuable enough so that some people will just walk away.

In closely held companies, allowing exercise of an option or the right to sell shares only upon sale of the company or an IPO is a very common approach. If a company allows exercise of an option or stock-settled SAR or allows restricted stock to vest before then, employees end up owning stock and having a tax obligation. Unless the company can provide a market for the shares (an issue discussed below), this combination may not seem like much of a reward. Companies and employees have to weigh just how likely these events are to occur, however. Management is often excessively optimistic about how marketable their company is.

It is also important to consider that if equity compensation awards all become exercisable upon sale or an IPO, buyers of the stock may not find the company so valuable. A minority of closely held companies are thus now restricting exercise to sometime after a sale or an IPO (in a sale situation, this requires the acquiring company to provide options in the new employer).

Finally, the plan design should be specific in its compliance with applicable securities laws and stock exchange rules that can restrict certain employees from exercising equity awards or selling stock acquired from them for a specified period around an IPO.

Providing a Market for the Shares

For publicly traded companies, providing a market for shares obtained through equity awards is not an issue, but for employees of closely held companies, it is one of the most important of all design issues. The majority of closely held companies solve the problem by limiting the exercise or sale of equity awards to when the company is sold or goes public. This makes sense for companies that realistically see these alternatives as likely to happen in the foreseeable future. Some company leaders, however, assume that they can *only* provide for marketability upon these events because a closely held company, for one reason or another, cannot provide a market itself. There are, in fact, alternatives for those companies and for companies that prefer to stay closely held and have no plans to sell or become public. These companies can provide an internal market by buying back the shares themselves; setting up an ESOP, which can buy the shares with pretax dollars through the ESOP trust; having employees sell to each other, with the company acting as a clearinghouse (but not itself buying shares) to let people know who is selling or who is buying; or, for companies willing to deal with the many securities law issues involved, setting up an internal stock market in which the company acts as a backup buyer in a market it runs for employee buyers and sellers.

Premium Pricing and Other Performance Bells and Whistles

Some companies are now looking at adding more performance triggers to their individual equity awards. As mentioned, vesting can be performance-triggered, as can the actual grant of awards (or the sizes of grants). In addition, companies can use premium-priced awards, such as issuing options at a grant price 10% above the current market price. In the executive compensation field, entire books have been written about formulas for basing equity awards on performance. Another idea growing in popularity is the indexed award, which either vests or is granted only if the company's stock outperforms its peers. The details of these approaches are beyond the scope of this book, however. Suffice it to say that picking a performance measure (EBITDA, economic value added, stock price growth, etc.) that really captures what the executive can actually make happen or what is best for the company overall, or both, can be tricky.

Purchasing vs. Grant

A key consideration for many employers is whether employees will have to pay anything for their equity. At one extreme are employers in closely held companies who see the chance to own stock as itself a valuable benefit, even if it is offered at fair market value. At the other are those who believe employees cannot or should not take the risk to invest in company stock, but do want them to have a stake in the company. Several considerations apply to any choice on this matter:

- *Do employees have the resources to buy stock?* If not, is the company willing to loan them the money? If the loan carries an interest rate below market rate, check with your attorney about possible tax implications.

- *How many employees will buy stock, either at full value or a discount?* The results are often disappointing and may not provide enough people with an equity stake to accomplish the "ownership culture" objectives the company hopes to achieve.

- *Even if a lot of employees buy shares, will the distribution of ownership be enough to create a real stake in the outcome for most people?* Employees whose financial obligations (or consumer preferences) leave them with little discretionary income, as well as employees who are risk-averse, may end up with only token amounts of stock.

- *If there is a discount, how much will it be?* Discounts of more than 15% usually result in taxable income to the employee, and even smaller discounts can have the same result if the payout date isn't scheduled well in advance (see the chapters on stock purchase plans and deferred compensation for details).

- *Is paying for an option good enough?* If an employee uses cash or shares to exercise an option, is that enough to satisfy the company's desire to have people buy shares, even though there is a certain gain for those who sell their shares immediately?

In most companies, widespread ownership does not occur solely through a stock purchase plan, even with incentives. ESPPs or other stock purchase arrangements might, therefore, be considered adjuncts to other plans. For some companies, however, broad ownership is not the goal. Rather, the objective is to engage specific employees and/or to raise capital.

One Vehicle or More

The different objectives and consequences of these varying approaches suggest that the best approach might be to combine one or more equity compensation vehicles. For instance, some kind of automatic grant that provides stock to most or all employees based on an equitable formula might serve as a base, with options or other individual equity awards provided to key employees and/or to exceptional performers at any level. An ESPP can round things out by allowing employees who do want larger ownership positions to obtain them.

Securities Law Issues

If employees are given a right to purchase shares, the offer is subject to securities laws. ESOPs and 401(k) plans are not subject to most securities law requirements unless employees have a right to buy shares. The trust serves as the shareholder of record in these plans, and its ownership counts as one shareholder no matter how many people participate in the plan.

The two key elements of securities laws are registration and disclosure. Registration means the filing of documents with the state and/or federal securities agencies concerning the employer whose stock is being sold. There are registration procedures for small offerings of stock (under $1 million or $5 million, depending on the procedure) that can be done for legal fees of as little as $10,000 in some cases, but larger offerings require a lot of complex paperwork, and fees often exceed $100,000. There are registration exemptions for broad offerings of stock to employees that meet certain rules, as well as for limited offerings to "accredited" investors, offers entirely within one state (but this applies only to federal registration rules), or offers to fewer than 35 people. Registration includes the filing of audited financial statements and continuing reporting obligations to the federal Securities and Exchange Commission (SEC) and appropriate state agencies.

Disclosure, which is not limited to companies that have registered their shares, refers to providing information to buyers about what they are getting, similar to, but frequently less detailed than, what would be in a prospectus. At times, specific state and federal rules dictate what needs to go in these documents, including objective discussions of risks, the financial condition of the firm, officers' and directors' compensation, and other information. In the absence of requirements for the registration of the securities, disclosure is intended to satisfy the anti-fraud requirements of federal and state laws.

Public companies must make sure their plan design complies with trading restrictions that apply to corporate insiders. This requires the filing of various reports and the restriction of some trading activity, among other things. These issues are too technical for adequate discussion here. Public companies should consult with their legal counsel on these matters before designing their plans.

Securities law issues are discussed in detail in a separate chapter in this book.

Conclusion

Designing an effective equity plan is a difficult balancing act. There are no perfect approaches. The financial and organizational significance of these plans demands that they be considered at least as carefully as any other major investment of company assets and time, not just picked at random or based on limited information. Try to talk to peers who have set up plans (the NCEO can help identify other companies with plans if you are a member), interview a few different consultants, read enough to feel comfortable with plan structures, and seek the input of board members and, preferably, employees into what kind of plan will work best—and be prepared to make changes as you learn more.

CHAPTER 11

Deciding on Executive Equity

COREY ROSEN

Over the last several years, executive compensation has become a major source of controversy. Reforms to accounting rules, the Sarbanes-Oxley Act, increased shareholder pressure to more closely align executive pay with corporate performance, and, for many people, a feeling that executive pay is simply too high relative to the pay of other employees all have put pressures on boards to make more considered decisions on how to pay their executives. Because equity compensation is often a major component of compensation at this level (and the largest share in many companies), particular attention must be paid to this issue.

Deciding on executive equity compensation demands balancing a number of objectives, including:

- *External equity:* What is required to attract, retain, and motivate employees given what they might be able to earn elsewhere?

- *Internal equity:* Is the compensation executives receive equitable relative to their contributions to corporate performance and when compared with the contributions of employees at other levels?

- *Effectiveness:* Do the form, amount, and structure of compensation actually result in the kind of behavior they are intended to produce in an economically efficient way?

In deciding on executive compensation, it is important to look at all the elements of pay. Regulations issued by the Securities and Exchange Commission in 2006 outline these elements and require they be disclosed to shareholders of publicly traded companies. While closely held companies do not have to follow these rules, the rules do provide useful guidance on how to construct descriptions of compensation that allow direct comparisons among executives.

It is also important to think through the overall strategy for both executive and work force compensation and how equity compensation fits into that picture. Should the emphasis be on short-term cash incentives to produce immediate results or long-term incentives to produce growth? Is the goal to maximize profits that can be distributed to owners or maximize share value? What dilution levels are acceptable to shareholders? If equity plans are broad-based, what sorts of organizational culture issues would be raised by giving executives a substantial share of that equity? Does the organizational culture stress team-based rewards or individual incentives? Does it focus on providing large incentives for top performers (at any level), or is the focus more "we're all in this together"?

In addition to all these strategic considerations, legal issues must be taken into account. Deferred compensation that does not conform to Section 409A of the Internal Revenue Code can mean substantial tax penalties for recipients of improperly structured incentive awards (see the separate chapter on this issue for details). Subchapter S ESOP companies have another Section 409 to master—409(p). These rules, designed to prevent excessive concentration of equity benefits to a small number of employees, impose tax penalties so severe that they will bankrupt most companies that do not comply (for details, see the NCEO book *S Corporation ESOPs*). Finally, especially in ESOP companies, but really in any company, boards have a fiduciary obligation to make sure overall executive compensation is "reasonable."

This chapter looks at some of the common issues that come up in executive equity decisions. It does not cover issues already covered in the chapter on designing equity compensation plans. That is, it does not look at the relative merits of different kinds of equity compensation. Nor does it look at tax and legal issues, which are also discussed in other chapters. Instead, it provides some general strategic guidance on how to evaluate executive equity compensation.

External Equity: Deciding How Stock-Based Compensation Compares to the Market

Traditionally, most boards and compensation consultants have focused primarily, and even exclusively, on measures of external fairness when setting executive equity pay. This is not a simple matter, however. Consider these (imaginary) scenarios:

- William is the new CFO of a FlexiTech, a privately held technology company. The board offers him 5,000 options as a new hire grant. William demurs. "My peers are getting more than that," he says. "According to a compensation survey I recently saw, CFOs of tech startups are getting an average of 10,000 options each." But the board notes that FlexiTech has been in business for several years and, unlike the startups, actually is making a profit. Its options, the board insists, are worth a lot more.

- Mary is coming in as the new HR director at FlexiTech. She's offered a package of 1,000 options and 500 restricted shares. Mary calculates that comes to 0.5% of the company's equity, which is less than the survey William gave her shows other HR directors get at startups. The board counters that 0.5% of FlexiTech is worth a lot more than 1% of the comparison companies because FlexiTech is worth a lot more.

- Sally is the new CEO of Fiber Cloth Products, an ESOP company. Sally is offered 2,000 phantom shares in the company as part of her first year's pay, plus another 1,000 shares per year if profit targets are met. Sally says her peers are getting twice as much equity in similar companies. Fiber Cloth's board agrees, but points out that Sally is not counting the stock she would get in the ESOP, which is being funded at 18% of pay, well above the usual for corporate contributions to retirement plans. Plus, the board notes, other Fiber Cloth employees would consider it unfair for her to get so much more because Fiber Cloth claims it prides itself on a culture of fairness.

- Marvin is the chief operating officer of Toggle Corp., a publicly traded manufacturing company. Marvin says he has had offers from both manufacturers and other companies to jump ship. He'd be given a much larger equity stake than he currently gets at Toggle. The board asks Marvin if those companies could match the well-established retirement, health care, deferred cash compensation, paid vacation, and other benefits Toggle offers.

- Sally is a division manager at MultiMake, a small holding company. Friends of hers, she says, can get very large equity grants if their divisions meet certain targets. Her grants are much smaller but do not depend on meeting any objectives. She'd like the board members to think about how much they would offer if she were willing to trade in the guarantees for a performance-based award.

- Newton is a controller for Personal Services, a successful ESOP company. He's not happy with the stock options he has because a recent survey of companies in the same size range showed that the average value of these options at grant is $75,000, and his are worth only $50,000. The board members say averages can lie. They point out that the median amount on the same survey was about the same as Newton's, but a couple of very large grants in two of the 100 companies surveyed skewed the averages upward.

The examples are just a few of many illustrations we could devise to show just how complicated this issue is. They do suggest, however, some common problems in determining equity pay, as described below.

Focusing solely on the number of shares: One of the most common discussions we at the NCEO have with companies is with the executive who wants to give employees (or the employee who wants to get) x number of options, restricted stock, or other form of equity. Sometimes, this desire is based on what the executive has heard from peers at other companies; often, it is just a nice, round number that seems appealing.

The problem with this approach is that the number in itself is meaningless, other than in some purely symbolic sense. Unless the number itself just makes me happy, what I want as an employee is the dollars the number ultimately can provide. Getting 10,000 options in a company with a stock value of $5, good growth prospects, and a low risk of failure is worth a lot more than 50,000 options in a company whose shares are $1 per share, whose growth prospects are uncertain, and whose future is risky. A good way to think about this is to look at the cost of the award companies now have to record on the income statement. This amount is based on a formula that attempts to quantify the present value of an award on the date of grant. It takes into account risk, volatility, dividends, the price of the shares, the terms of the award, and general economic factors. It can compare the apples of options to the oranges of restricted stock to the plums of phantom stock as well. Armed with this number, companies have a much better sense of how to equate awards across companies.

Unfortunately, this is a little tricky for comparisons with closely held companies. For public companies, new SEC disclosure requirements, plus company financial statements, make it possible to compare grant values for at least the top five executives. Closely held companies, however, do not have to make this information public. Equity compensation surveys often only report either the number of awards granted or the percentage of the company's equity that represents. Nonetheless, the grant date value still can be added to other forms of pay and benefits to produce a total compensation number that gives a better picture of actual compensation.

Comparing percentages of shares owned: This is a very similar problem, but with more emotional zing. Being able to say you own x percent of a company has a certain resonance, even if the "percentage of what value?" factor is ignored (as it often is). But would you rather own 1% of a small, uncertain company or 0.0001% of Google? Furthermore, comparing percentages can be misleading because, say, a 2%

grant at an early-stage startup that then issues more shares in later rounds of funding can get diluted to 1%, whereas in an established company, 1% ownership is likely to remain roughly 1% ownership. So even the percentage itself cannot be compared from company to company unless they're at the same stage and anticipate the same future dilution due to rounds of venture capital funding or an IPO, which is a real guess.[1] Our best advice on using the percentage of the company owned as a measure is simple: don't, even if you see it done all the time.

Cherry-picking comparisons: You may have seen those ads for a lower-priced car that accelerates faster than a Saab, has more leg room than a BMW, gets better mileage than a Jaguar, and handles curves better than a Porsche (or some such marketing wizardry). You also know to be skeptical. You buy the whole car; you don't assemble components. Yet we see the same specious comparisons being made in equity pay all the time. "The surveys show the people in my position get more (fill in the blank) than I do," they say. But what they don't say is what else these people get or what risks are associated with those awards.

Not thinking through the risk-reward balance: One of the trickiest comparisons to make is between awards that are fairly certain, such as time-vested restricted stock or stock appreciation rights (SARs) granted every year as a percentage of pay, and ones that are not, such as performance vested or performance awarded equity. A well-schooled financial advisor may be able to calculate how the risks compare. It is, however, an inexact science. The value of an award to an employee really has two elements: how likely the company, group, or individual is to hit the target; and how the employees discount risk. Employees who have a high risk tolerance are going to value the same contingent level of pay more highly than those

---

1.   Even comparing percentages from one point to another within the same company can be misleading. Say an early-stage startup company makes a 1% of equity grant to a CFO then issues more shares in later rounds of funding. Now that 1% is diluted to 0.5%. So does the next named executive get 1% or 0.5%?

with a lower tolerance. The result is that paying exactly the same award to different people may be perceived in very different ways and have a very different impact on how fairly they think they are being paid.

Being misled by the law of averages: No, not that one. The law we have in mind is the one that says that in any distribution of compensation, the mean (average) is higher than the median (the point at which 50% are paid more). It has to be that way. There is an absolute bottom for employee pay—the minimum legal wage. The same holds true for equity compensation, but even more dramatically. Cash compensation may have no theoretical limits, but it usually doesn't top several million dollars. But equity awards can be hundreds of millions. Meanwhile, the vast majority of employees get either zero or not very much in equity. Michael Eisner and 10,000 ordinary Disney employees had a pretty decent average pay and equity compensation package, even though only Eisner got any equity and most employees didn't get a lot more than the minimum wage. Medians provide much more reliable numbers.

Internal Equity

The bad news is that comparing the external equity of stock-based compensation plans is monstrously complicated. The worse news is that it is easier than figuring out how to mesh that with a concept that is gaining a lot of traction in thinking about executive compensation, and particularly equity compensation: internal equity.

Internal equity is a way to measure how compensation balances the relative contributions of employees at differently levels. There are two very powerful arguments for it. First, it just makes sense to base pay on how much value each person adds. Why should a CEO get 20 times what the CFO gets when the CEO's contribution is not 20 times as great? Or 100 times what the top technical people get if the contribution is similarly not that different?

Second, perceived fairness in compensation is a huge issue in employee motivation, larger than most people have traditionally thought. While employee surveys have always shown that pay equity ranks very high on employee job satisfaction and turnover measures, economists have always assumed (and market analysts and boards have always argued) that if an executive gets an outsized pay package, but the company does well enough to provide job security and raises for everyone else, employees will be happy with the tradeoff. After all, classical economics assumes that a dollar is a dollar, and that an extra dollar is always a good thing. But a school of thought called behavioral economics has proven this theory wrong. In a series of Nobel Prize-winning experiments, scholars found that, among other things, employees are willing to give up economic gain to preserve fairness. [2]

For instance, two people are told they can split $10, but have to agree on how. If one person proposes an equal split, it's easily accepted. But as the split moves away from that, say to $7 and $3 or to $8 and $2, people offered the smaller portion say no, even though it means they won't get anything. Similarly, people are put in a game where they are betting against one another. The gist of the experiment is to see whether people will give up certain gains to punish someone they see as cheating. They generally do. Researchers have gone even further, doing MRI analyses of people while playing these games. Areas of the brain that show strong emotion light up like firecrackers when there is perceived unfairness. The explanation has roots in evolutionary psychology, essentially that punishing people who don't cooperate is essential for the long-term survival of a group.

All this helps explain why perceived fairness is so important, even if it is arguably irrational economically. Paying a top executive (or any other employee) what some metric might say they deserve, but that nonetheless is perceived as excessive by others, can result in substantial demotivation and higher turnover rates.

If you buy this argument (and many compensation consultants, regretfully, still don't), then the question becomes how to measure

---

2.   Daniel Kahneman of Princeton University and Amos Tversky of Stanford University demonstrated this and other seemingly irrational behaviors in their work on behavioral economics. Kahneman won the 2002 Nobel Prize in Economics for their work. (Tversky died in 1996. Nobel Prizes are not granted posthumously.)

relative contribution. One suggested approach is to restrict top executives' equity grants to a specific multiple of those given to employees at lower levels. So if the sales manager gets 1,000 options, the CFO will get some multiple of that based on a company judgment about their relative contributions to the company. Just how much lower the comparison group should be varies from one company to another. Many argue this should focus just on senior management; others argue this approach can work throughout the company. The notion is that pay for levels below the very top executives is more clearly driven by larger market forces (because there are more people at these levels and less noise—executive influence on boards in particular—in setting pay rates) and thus this serves as a good test of what a job is worth.

Two caveats are important here. First, fairness almost never means the same thing to everyone. People see "fair" in terms of whether they believe that they are paid fairly given what they contribute to the company and relative to what others are paid given their contributions. Alas, this is subject to the Lake Wobegon effect—we all think we are above average. Results-based fairness is thus pretty tricky, even if you cannot ignore it. Equally important is process-based fairness. Do employees think the way in which performance is measured accurately assesses how well they have done? Companies that can be more transparent about how executive contributions to the company are measured and rewarded—and that can create well-thought-out rationales—have a considerable leg up. Second, internal equity cannot be the sole driver of compensation. A plan may be perfect in these terms, but if executives believe they are getting a bad deal, the risk of their leaving is greater. Like all the issues raised here, delicate balancing is needed.

Effectiveness

A final set of issues to consider involves effectiveness. Does the equity compensation system actually deliver what it is intended to do?

The first question is: Just what is it intended to do? The typical answer is to "attract, retain, and motivate employees." That's hard to argue with, but not all that helpful. For instance, say you have an executive who has been with the company for a while and loves her job. It provides responsibilities that match her talents, it offers a good work-life balance, she likes the people she works with, and the company has a great and productive culture. All of these things have been shown to be very highly correlated with motivation and retention—more highly correlated, in fact, than most compensation issues.

Perhaps this executive notices that people at other companies can make more. But she'd have to move and uproot her family, work for a company whose culture may not be so appealing, and take a job whose responsibilities are similar to, but not quite as good a match for her talents as, her current job. Her stock awards could be increased, but would they really affect her decision to stay or not stay? Would she really work any less hard or effectively? If the answer is no, then paying more is not an efficient use of resources. A board may do it anyway, perhaps just because it seems fairer, but that means those resources are not available for other uses.

A much more difficult set of issues revolves around whether the equity incentive rewards the right kind of behavior. Many people argued that the outsized equity grants to CEOs and other top executives of large companies in recent years encouraged excessive risk-taking and short-term thinking. The nature of an option or SAR is that the more volatile the stock, the more valuable the award. Imagine two companies with an average 12% return over five years. One varies only slightly from that each year; the other goes up 20% in one year, down 15% in the next, up 30% the next, etc. The option in the second case is worth much more because the executive can exercise and sell the stock at the highs and ignore the option at the lows. In formulas for valuing options, volatility is often the key factor in determining value. A profit-maximizing executive would readily conclude that the best idea would be to take a lot of risks and push for short-term gains that might have negative long-term implications.

Restricted stock and phantom stock may seem like a solution, especially if they have long-term vesting, or, better, long-term performance vesting. But shareholders hated restricted stock back in the early 1990s, when it was last popular. It was "pay for pulse," they said.

Another issue is how the awards are issued and vested. Performance-based vesting seems ideal on the surface, but by what measure? Stock prices can be influenced by a lot of factors not specific to company performance. Indexing against comparable companies helps ease this problem, but may not be a very helpful solution for closely held companies where comparable company data are hard to get. Even if a good measure can be constructed, there is still an issue of whether an executive other than the CEO should be held responsible for it. What about a division vice-president whose division does well, but whose company does not? Or an HR director who does a fabulous job of improving compliance and creating an ownership culture, but who works for a company that has made some bad marketing decisions? On the other hand, creating the right measures of performance is not easy, and the wrong measures could cause executives to focus excessively on those things at the cost of working on matters that help the company overall.

Effectiveness is also a function of how different individuals assess risk, as mentioned earlier. Studies show that, in general, employees value options at a substantial discount to the amount arrived at using option-pricing models. Just how large a discount varies from person to person. Moreover, the marginal value of more dollars declines with each extra dollar, just like the marginal value of one more piece of pizza does. When you're paid a lot, it takes a lot more to create motivation. For a $40,000 per year employee, another $10,000 is a big deal. For a $400,000 employee, the extra $10,000 is not as critical.

All of these things are very difficult to assess, and we have no magic-bullet solutions. But even educated guesses are better than formulaic and poorly considered assumptions.

Purchasing and Holding

Many companies want executives to buy stock and/or hold onto shares for at least some period of time after an equity award is exercised (other than shares that need to be sold for paying taxes or other specified purposes). In fact, some companies impose holding requirements as part of their equity grants. However, there is not any compelling research on whether this makes any difference in employee behaviors so this is largely a matter of corporate philosophy.

Conclusions

We wish we could provide some simple answers to these questions, but it would be presumptuous and misleading to do so. Every company is different, and each company needs to look to its own circumstances to decide. What we hope this can help boards do, however, is know the key issues—and understand the complex balancing that needs to take place—rather than rely on the often simplistic rules of thumb that frequently govern this issue.

Viewing the Webinar on Equity Sharing

The CD attached to the inside back cover of this book includes a prerecorded Webinar (an audiovisual presentation viewed through a Web browser) by coauthor Corey Rosen on sharing equity with employees through stock options, restricted stock, phantom stock, stock appreciation rights, and other means.

How to View the Webinar

To view the Webinar, insert the CD in your computer. If your computer does not automatically start playing the presentation, it may give you a prompt, offering to play the content on the disc. Alternatively, navigate to the CD (either via your operating system, such as Windows Explorer or My Computer on Windows, or in your Web browser's "Open" or "Open File" function) and double-click the "index.htm" file in the root folder of the CD (in some operating systems, "index.htm" may appear simply as "index"). The Webinar will them begin playing, provided that your computer has Flash installed; see "System Requirements" below.

If your Web browser does not start playing the Webinar but instead warns you (for example, Internet Explorer may flash a yellow bar at the top of the screen stating, "Internet Explorer has restricted this webpage from running scripts or ActiveX controls that could access your computer"), follow the browser's prompts to play the content on the CD.

System Requirements

You will need a computer with a CD player and a Web browser (such as Internet Explorer or Firefox). You do not have to be connected to the Internet. However, your computer must have Flash Player (software to play multimedia content) installed; in almost all cases, it already is. If Flash is not already installed, your browser may prompt you to install it, or you can go to www.adobe.com and manually install Flash Player (a free download).

How to Use the Webinar Player

When the Webinar plays in your Web browser, it includes a succession of slides in the main portion of the screen, a vertical column of thumbnails on the left that you can show or hide, and a small player window on top with standard playback functions. To jump to a specific portion of the recording, you may scroll vertically through the thumbnails and click the thumbnail that corresponds to the portion of the recording you wish to view. Alternatively, you can use the controls in the player window to move through the presentation. To show the vertical thumbnails on the left-hand portion of your browser window, click the curved tab on the left. The thumbnails will disappear when not in use.

Show/Hide Player

To hide the player window (not the presentation but rather the playback controller), click on the minimize button near the top right-hand corner of the player window. The player will fade away; in its place, a tiny window with stop, pause, and play buttons will appear in the top-left area of the browser screen. To show the player again, click on your browser screen or in the gray area to the left of the stop/pause/play buttons. The player will reappear.

Exiting the Presentation

To stop viewing the recording and exit from the player, close your browser window.

About the Authors

Three of this book's authors are from the National Center for Employee Ownership (NCEO), a private, nonprofit membership, information, and research organization in Oakland, CA. The NCEO is widely considered to be the authoritative source on broad-based employee ownership plans.

Pam Chernoff, CEP, is the NCEO's director of equity compensation projects. She is the editor of *The Stock Options Book,* writes for NCEO publications, and coordinates the content for the NCEO's prep course for the Certified Equity Professional exam. She was previously an editor at *Pensions & Investments* newspaper and has a master's degree in journalism from Northwestern University.

Daniel N. Janich is the managing principal of Janich Law Group. He has extensive experience counseling businesses and executives on all aspects of employee benefits and executive compensation, including tax, securities law, and ERISA. He also litigates employee benefits and executive compensation claims. A former chair of the Chicago Bar Association's Employee Benefits Committee, Mr. Janich is currently associate senior editor of *Employee Benefits Law* and management co-chair of the Reporting and Disclosure Subcommittee of the ABA Labor and Employment Law Section's Employee Benefits Committee. He is also a Fellow of the American College of Employee Benefits Counsel. Mr. Janich received a B.A. degree cum laude in history from Marian College, Indianapolis; a J.D. degree from The John Marshall Law School, Chicago; and an LL.M. in Taxation degree from DePaul University, Chicago.

Scott Rodrick is the NCEO's director of publishing and information technology. He designed and created the NCEO's present line of publications and is the author or coauthor of several books himself, including the best-selling *An Introduction to ESOPs* (8th ed. 2007). He is the editor of the *Journal of Employee Ownership Law and Finance,* the only professional journal in the English language devoted to employee stock plans. Since 1994, he has created and maintained the NCEO's presence on the Internet. He is an attorney and served at the U.S. Department of Labor as an attorney-advisor before coming to the NCEO.

Corey Rosen is the NCEO's executive director. He cofounded the NCEO in 1981 after working for five years as a professional staff member in the U.S. Senate, where he helped draft legislation on employee ownership plans. Before that, he taught political science at Ripon College. He is the author or coauthor of many books and over 100 articles on employee ownership, and coauthor (with John Case and Martin Staubus) of *Equity: Why Employee Ownership Is Good for Business* (Harvard Business School Press, 2005). He was the subject of an extensive interview in *Inc.* magazine in August 2000; has appeared frequently on CNN, PBS, NPR, and other network programs; and is regularly quoted in the *Wall Street Journal,* the *New York Times,* and other leading publications. He has a Ph.D. in political science from Cornell University and serves on the advisory board of the Certified Equity Professional Institute. He also serves on the board of directors of the Great Place to Work Institute, creator of *Fortune* magazine's "100 Best Companies to Work for in America" list.

About the NCEO

The National Center for Employee Ownership (NCEO) is widely considered to be the leading authority in employee ownership in the U.S. and the world. Established in 1981 as a nonprofit information and membership organization, it now has over 2,500 members, including companies, professionals, unions, government officials, academics, and interested individuals. It is funded entirely through the work it does.

The NCEO's mission is to provide the most objective, reliable information possible about employee ownership at the most affordable price possible. As part of the NCEO's commitment to providing objective information, it does not lobby or provide ongoing consulting services. The NCEO publishes a variety of materials on employee ownership and participation, provides online education, and holds dozens of seminars, Webinars, and conferences on employee ownership annually. The NCEO's work includes extensive contacts with the media, both through articles written for trade and professional publications and through interviews with reporters. It has written or edited five books for outside publishers during the past two decades. Finally, the NCEO maintains an extensive Web site at www.nceo.org.

See below for information on membership benefits and fees. To join, see the order form at the end of this section, visit our Web site at www.nceo.org, or telephone us at 510-208-1300.

Selected NCEO Publications

The NCEO offers a variety of publications on all aspects of employee ownership and participation. Following are descriptions of a few of our main publications. We publish new books and revise old ones on a yearly basis. To obtain the most current information on what we have available, visit our extensive Web site at www.nceo.org or call us at 510-208-1300.

Equity Compensation Plans

- This book, *The Decision-Maker's Guide to Equity Compensation,* explains how equity compensation plans work and what the considerations are for choosing and designing them.

  $35 for NCEO members, $50 for nonmembers

- *The Stock Options Book* is a straightforward, comprehensive overview covering the legal, accounting, regulatory, and design issues involved in implementing a stock option or stock purchase plan.

  $25 for NCEO members, $35 for nonmembers

- *Beyond Stock Options* is a complete guide, including annotated model plans, to phantom stock, restricted stock, stock appreciation rights, performance awards, and more. Includes a CD with plan documents.

  Price: $35 for NCEO members, $50 for nonmembers

- *Accounting for Equity Compensation* is a guide to the financial accounting rules that govern equity compensation programs in the United States.

  $35 for NCEO members, $50 for nonmembers

Employee Stock Ownership Plans (ESOPs)

- *The ESOP Reader* is an overview of the issues involved in establishing and operating an ESOP. It covers the basics of ESOP rules, feasibility, valuation, and other matters, and then discusses managing an ESOP company, including brief case studies.

  $25 for NCEO members, $35 for nonmembers

- *Selling to an ESOP* is a detailed guide for owners, managers, and advisors of closely held businesses. It explains how ESOPs work and then offers a comprehensive look at legal structures, valuation, financing (including self-financing), and other matters, especially the tax-deferred section 1042 "rollover" that allows owners to indefinitely defer capital gains taxation on the sale proceeds.

$25 for NCEO members, $35 for nonmembers

- *ESOPs and Corporate Governance* covers everything from shareholder rights to the impact of Sarbanes-Oxley to choosing a fiduciary.

  $25 for NCEO members, $35 for nonmembers

- *ESOP Valuation* brings together and updates where needed the best articles on ESOP valuation that we have published in our *Journal of Employee Ownership Law and Finance,* described below.

  $25 for NCEO members, $35 for nonmembers

- *Executive Compensation in ESOP Companies* discusses executive compensation issues, special ESOP considerations, and the first-ever survey of executive compensation in ESOP companies.

  $25 for NCEO members, $35 for nonmembers

Other

- *Section 401(k) Plans and Employee Ownership* focuses on how company stock is used in 401(k) plans, both in stand-alone 401(k) plans and combination 401(k)–ESOP plans ("KSOPs").

  $25 for NCEO members, $35 for nonmembers

To join the NCEO as a member or to order any of the publications listed on the preceding pages, use the order form on the following page, use the secure ordering system on our Web site at www.nceo.org, or call us at 510-208-1300. If you join at the same time you order publications, you will receive the members-only publication discounts.

Order Form

To order, fill out this form and mail it with your credit card information or check to the NCEO at 1736 Franklin St., 8th Flr., Oakland, CA 94612; fax it with your credit card information to the NCEO at 510-272-9510; telephone us at 510-208-1300 with your credit card in hand; or order at our Web site, www.nceo.org. If you are not already a member, you can join now to receive member discounts on any publications you order.

Name

Organization

Address

City, State, Zip (Country)

Telephone   Fax   E-mail

Method of Payment: ❏ Check (payable to "NCEO")   ❏ Visa   ❏ M/C   ❏ AMEX

Credit Card Number

Signature   Exp. Date

Checks are accepted only for orders from the U.S. and must be in U.S. currency.

Title	Qty.	Price	Total

Subtotal	$	
Sales Tax	$	
Shipping	$	
Membership	$	
TOTAL DUE	$	

Tax: California residents add 8.75% sales tax (on publications only, not membership or Journal subscriptions)

Shipping: In the U.S., first publication $5, each add'l $1; elsewhere, we charge exact shipping costs to your credit card, plus (except for Canada) a $10 handling surcharge; no shipping charges for membership or Journal subscriptions

Introductory NCEO Membership: $80 for one year ($90 outside the U.S.)